Mama's Boarding House

Life in the South
During the Great Depression

By

Sidney Bolick

With Illustrations By
Anita Bolick

Canadian Cataloguing in Publication Data

Bolick, Sidney, 1924-
  Mama's boarding house

ISBN 1-55212-517-3

1. Bolick, Sidney, 1924- 2. North Carolina--Biography. I. Title.
F259.B64A3 2000   975.6'042'092C00-911267-7

TRAFFORD

This book was published *on-demand* in cooperation with Trafford Publishing.
On-demand publishing is a unique process and service of making a book available for retail
sale to the public taking advantage of on-demand manufacturing and Internet marketing.
On-demand publishing includes promotions, retail sales, manufacturing, order fulfilment,
accounting and collecting royalties on behalf of the author.

Suite 6E, 2333 Government St., Victoria, B.C. V8T 4P4, CANADA
Phone   250-383-6864   Toll-free   1-888-232-4444 (Canada & US)
Fax   250-383-6804   E-mail   sales@trafford.com
Web site   www.trafford.com   TRAFFORD PUBLISHING IS A DIVISION OF TRAFFORD HOLDINGS LTD.
Trafford Catalogue #00-0182   www.trafford.com/robots/00-0182.html

10   9   8   7   6   5   4   3

Thanks

To Dot and Betsy, and the rest of the staff at the Mildred G. Fields Memorial Library, for their help and encouragement in the writing of this book; and to the residents of Milan Residential Care Center, who listened to the first reading of the manuscript and liked it enough to suggest that I try to get it published.

To Ella Mae, Belle, Jake, George and Dot, for helping me research our family's history.

Most of all, thanks and love to my wife, Anita, who not only did the illustrations for the book, but read each page as it was written, edited my mistakes, and offered good, constructive comments and criticisms.

S. B.

Contents

Foreword

By the middle of the year nineteen-thirty-one, when I was seven years old, the United States was beginning to feel the full effect of what history would call the "Great Depression of the Nineteen Thirties". As an aftermath of the stock market crash of October, 1929, banks failed, factories closed, farmers lost their farms, and unemployment was approaching an all time high. Breadlines and soup kitchens sprouted on street corners in the cities, and freight trains were festooned with hobos aimlessly traveling from one part of the country to the other to try to find work. But there was almost no work to be had.

Just about everybody blamed the depression on Republican President Herbert Hoover. And he was easy to blame. Unlike his eventual successor, Franklin D. Roosevelt, he was not a charismatic individual, but projected an aloof and unsympathetic demeanor. Even his physical appearance was against him, with his squinted eyes and severe facial expression.

But the depression wasn't Hoover's fault. It was a worldwide phenomenon, brought about by a combination of economic and political conditions after World War I. He just had the misfortune of coming into office at the wrong time.

Looking back on those years, I might be expected to say that they were the worst years of my life. But that was not true. Certainly, times were hard, and we had to scratch for everything we got. But I never once went hungry, and always had a warm bed to sleep in and enough clothes to wear. If the clothes were hand-me-downs from an older brother, they were always clean and pressed and neatly mended. And I was a part of a large, close-knit family, where everyone pulled his weight and contributed his share to the common kitty. Two of my older brothers managed to find part-time jobs even during the worst of the depression, and Daddy worked a day or two a week on the WPA. And when I was ten years old, Mama took in boarders to supplement the family income.

In spite of the hard times, and the need to earn extra money to help out the family, I still managed to have a pretty normal childhood and do most of the things that young boys do as they are growing up. I had crushes on the little girls in grade school, and fell madly in love several times in my early teens. I learned to swim in the old muddy South Fork River before I was ten years old, played baseball on a red clay field with a taped-up broken bat and a friction-tape-covered ball, and tennis on a rundown court with a string tied across between two posts to serve as a net. When I was twelve I joined the Boys Scouts and worked up to the rank of Life Scout before quitting to work in the mill when I reached sixteen.

I shot marbles for keeps in a circle drawn in the dirt, made slingshots out of strips from old rubber inner tubes and prongs from the forked branches of a dogwood tree, with which I terrorized the stray dogs and cats in the neighborhood. I also learned to spin a top and play mumbly peg with a two bladed jack knife without losing a finger. And on the more useful side, I sawed and split firewood for Mama's woodburning cookstove, fed the chickens and collected the eggs, and helped Daddy in the big kitchen garden that he planted every year.

So the stories in this book are not just about hard times and deprivation, but are real-life memories of the people I knew, and things I experienced, while growing up in the South during a time unlike any other in this country's history. And some of the best of these are the memories of Mama's Boarding House.

Part One

Childhood On The Farm

1

Earliest Memories

One of my earliest memories is of playing in the yard with my nephew, Bob. His name was actually Willie Robert, but his Mama was the only one who called him that. He was my Mama's oldest grandchild, and my sister Ella Mae's firstborn. I was about three and a half and Bob was a year younger. I remember it because he hit me on one of my bare toes with a rock and the nail came off.

The yard we were playing in was in front of the house we lived in that year. It was on land that my Daddy farmed on shares for the owner, Judge Owens, near the little town of Fountain Inn, South Carolina. Judge Owens probably wasn't a real judge, but had acquired the title as a mark of respect since he was one of the biggest landowners in the county. Just like a lot of well-to-do Southerners were called, "Cap'n", even though they had never been in the army. In addition to my Daddy and Ella Mae's husband, Woody Lankford, the Judge had two other families of tenant farmers, another white family and one colored family, sharecropping on farmland that he owned. He supplied the land, some sort of rudimentary dwelling, a barn, plows, and other farming equipment, as well as the seed for planting the cotton and corn, and the fertilizer for growing it. The tenants supplied mules and human labor.

The landowner also advanced money to his tenants during the winter months for food, fuel and clothing, and deducted it from their share of the proceeds when the crops were harvested. Since these advances usually equaled or exceeded the tenant's share of the crop, they ended up in debt to him at the end of the year, and were bound by contract to farm his land again the next year. This would go on for two or three years until a bumper crop or high cotton prices allowed the tenant to pay off his debt. At which time he would usually move on in search of greener pastures and another landlord. Counting the place where I was born, near Oglethorpe, Georgia, we lived on three different farms by the time I was six years old.

This house was better than some we had lived in. It was a rectangular box with roughsawed siding that had been painted white at sometime in the past, but most of the paint had flaked off, leaving it a sort of dirty gray color. It had a planked roof covered with shingles, and stood about two feet off the ground on blocks cut from tree trunks, providing a dim cool place for animals to hide or little boys to play, and for Mama to store the glass jars of fruits and vegetables that she canned in the summer. Three wooden steps led up to a much-patched screen door that fought a losing battle against the flies and mosquitoes.

About half the inside of the house was taken up by one big room. The wooden planked floors were covered with cheap linoleum rugs that cracked and broke where the planks didn't quite fit together, and had been scrubbed so many times that the original floral pattern had faded to an indistinct blur. A big potbellied cast iron stove stood on its square tin floor mat at one end of the room, its stovepipe chimney reaching up to a flue in the ceiling. It burned wood and provided all the heat and most of the light for the whole house during the winter.

Our house on the Owens place

The rest of the room was dominated by a long table covered with white oilcloth. It had a bench along the length of either side, a straight-backed chair at each end, and a cut-glass kerosene lamp in the center. It served not only as a dining table, but as the center of activity for the whole family. The older kids did their homework on it, while Daddy laboriously read the weekly newspaper and Mama wrote her infrequent letters to her Mama in North Carolina. Two more kerosene lamps stood on their shelves on either side of the room, and a few assorted chairs and stools completed the austere furnishings.

Part of the ceiling was floored over to make a sleeping loft that was reached by a ladder against the wall at one side of the room. This was where the older boys - Hays, 16; Fred, 14; and Jake, 9, slept. The loft had no ceiling, just the bare rafters and roofing. Cracks in the wood and shingle roof let the boys lie on their backs and look up at the stars on clear nights, but also let the water drip on them when it rained. Mama and my sister Belle pasted pages torn from Spiegels and Sears, Roebuck catalogs on the walls to provide a rudimentary insulation. It was stifling hot under the roof in the summer, and cold in the winter, but from the time I was able to walk I looked forward to the day when I would be old enough to climb the ladder and sleep with the big boys.

A sort of lean-to ran the length of the back of the house, and was divided into the kitchen and two small bedrooms. My Mama and Daddy slept in one of the bedrooms, and Belle and me in the other. These rooms were separated from each other by a kind of wallboard made of pressed paper, which provided only an illusion of privacy, since any noise above a whisper could be heard throughout the house.

The kitchen was primitive by today's standards. Since we had no electricity, there was no pump to provide running water from the well in the back yard. Water for cooking had to be carried from the well up the steps and through the back door, then poured into the big reservoir on one end of the woodburning cook stove where it was heated for washing dishes and for our weekly baths.

Another, smaller, wooden table occupied the middle of the kitchen. It was covered by the same white oilcloth, and surrounded by walls that were lined with wooden shelves for dishes, and hooks for pots and pans. Mama had made curtains out of sugar sacks and flour sacks dyed with Rit Dye, and had put them on drawstrings over the shelves that held her dishes, to protect them from dust. An ancient handmade two-drawer chest sat at one end of the kitchen next to the galvanized tin sink, and held cooking utensils and table cutlery. Like all Mama's houses, the kitchen and all the rest of the house was spotlessly clean.

The house sat on the red clay soil indigenous to that part of the South, among a few scrub pine trees that provided scant shade from the hot summer sun, but gave off an aroma of pine needles and pinetar and rosin that helped to disguise the odors from the nearby barn and pigsty, and the outdoor privy at the end of a well worn path behind the house. The barn itself was a ramshackle affair that had been thrown together out of whatever spare material that was available, including tin signs for Mail Pouch chewing tobacco and Lydia Pinkham's Nerve Tonic. It gave shelter to our two old mules, our milk cow and Mama's chickens, as well as storage for the plows and other farm equipment. It had a hayloft of sorts, and when we were old enough to climb the ladder, Bob and I spent many happy hours tunneling through the hay that was stored there to feed the mules.

Ella Mae and Woody's house was down the hill near the creek, and was a smaller carbon copy of ours, except that it had a corrugated tin roof, instead of one made of boards and shingles. It also had a sleeping loft, and I will always remember the sound of the rain on that tin roof. It was a peaceful, rhythmic sound that was almost hypnotic, and it quickly lulled us to sleep in spite of an occasional drop of water that fell on us through a rusty nail hole.

The creek that ran by the house was clean enough for swimming, in those pre-pollution days of the nineteen-twenties, although its water had a reddish brown color from the soil of its banks and bottom. It was one of the few sources of fun and relaxation for my older brothers, who had little enough time for fun, between going to school and working on the farm with Daddy.

They had built a partial dam across it at a narrow point, using old logs and brush, creating a pool that was perfect for swimming and cooling the watermelons that we "swiped" from Woody's patch. No watermelon since has ever tasted as good as those did when we took them cold from the creek and dropped them on the bank and ate the sweet red centers with our bare hands. Of course, Woody knew we were taking them, but he never let on, as that would have spoiled the fun of it.

Bob and I weren't old enough to swim in the pool, but after covering ourselves with watermelon juice we splashed in the creek to wash ourselves off.

Looking back now I can see that those were good years for me, those warm summers among the South Carolina pines and the cozy winters around the big stove, with Mama reading to us from the Bible Story Book that was illustrated with all the pretty, if sometimes scary, pictures. We were very poor, and any toys that we had were handmade, not store bought, and it was a rare occasion when Daddy had a spare penny to buy me a stick of hard candy at the General Store on one of his trips to town. But

SIDNEY BOLICK

it's true that you don't miss what you've never had, and I
was a happy little boy in those days before we left the farm
and moved to town.

2

Sarah Jane and Sidney

My mother and father were married in the year 1905. He was eighteen and she was fourteen. This was not unusual at that time in the mountains of Appalachia, where boys were considered to be men at sixteen, and girls were prospective brides anytime after reaching puberty, if they were physically mature enough.

Mama was born Sarah Jane Ash, the eldest daughter and second oldest of the ten children of Coleman and Callie Ash. Grandpa Ash owned and farmed a few acres of land on the slopes of a mountain near Sylva, North Carolina . He had tried growing various crops, including tobacco, but none of them took to the poor soil on the rocky mountainside slopes. He finally settled on raising hogs and a few cattle, and growing corn to feed them. At some point he discovered that corn produced a better return when used to make corn likker, and if he didn't actually become a moonshiner he certainly supplied some of them with the raw material for their stills.

Since Grandpa Ash's most abundant crop was children, my mother had three or four younger brothers and sisters to look after by the time she was six years old. Life was hard on a mountain farm, and everybody worked from the time they were able to walk. The men and boys cleared the land, tilled the soil, planted, cultivated and harvested the crops, herded the cattle, butchered the hogs, and when that was all done they tramped the hills and valleys with a twenty-two rifle, hunting for squirrels or rabbits or grouse for the table. The women and girls cooked, carried water from the mountain spring to the house, cleaned the house, washed the clothes, milked the cows, slopped the hogs, fed the chickens, looked after the babies and young children, planted and tended the kitchen garden, picked wild berries and fruit and canned it in half-gallon Mason jars along with vegetables from the garden, to be eaten during the cold mountain winter.

It was no wonder then, that by the time she was twelve years old, my mother was beginning to dream of getting away from all the drudgery and having a home of her own, where she could be her own boss and do as she pleased. The fact that she would have to have a husband in order to do this seemed like a minor inconvenience at the time. At age thirteen she was a fully developed woman, big for her age, pretty, and mature beyond her years. So when my Daddy came across from the next mountain to pay court to her, she did not reject his attentions.

My father, Sidney Rose Bolick, was the sixth and last child of John A. Bolick and Louise George Bolick. John Bolick, a schoolteacher and the son of German immigrant Gabriel Bolick, died of pneumonia at the age of thirty-four, seven months before my father was born. Ironically, he had ordered a Seth Thomas Grandfathers' clock before his death and it arrived after he died, just about the time my father was born. Grandma Bolick sold a cow to pay for it. It was given to Daddy as a wedding present by his mother, and became a cherished family possession. Since I was his namesake, he promised it to me when he died, but it was destroyed when our family house burned down right after World War II.

Unable to raise six children by herself after my grandfather's death, my grandmother remarried, to a man named Elbert Bryson, and bore him six more children.

Mama and Daddy in the year 1905

Although from all accounts she tried to be fair and impartial to all her children, my father, as he grew up, found himself caught more and more in the middle, being the youngest of the Bolick children and older than his Bryson half brothers and sisters. By the time he was in his teens his older siblings were growing up and leaving home, and while there is no record of his having gotten into any serious trouble, I remember some talk among my older aunts and uncles about him being a little wild. When he met my mother he was still living at home and working on his stepfather's farm, but he, too, was ready to leave the nest and start a family of his own. They were married in June, 1905.

When I think of my Daddy I remember him as a quiet, gentle and kind man, who worked hard and turned his pay envelope over to my mother every week, after taking out a few cents for his weekly supply of chewing tobacco. He didn't drink or gamble, and I can't remember ever hearing him raise his voice in anger. But I guess he hadn't always been that way. My mother never complained to us about our father, but as I grew older I was able to put together a picture of their early married life from little things that she said and from listening to talk between her and my older sisters and aunts.

I believe my Daddy loved my Mama from the first moment he saw her until the day he died. But when they were first married he felt it was his place to be the man of the house, the king of his own castle, and he behaved accordingly. She put up with it for a long time, since that was the way she had been raised, and she soon had babies to think about and care for. But somewhere along the way she got tired of the careless, and often foolish, way he handled the family's finances, and put her foot down. From that point on she took over the reins and managed the family affairs with a firm hand. I don't remember it being any other way. As I was growing up it was Mama who handled the household finances and paid the bills and bought the food and clothing. And it was Mama, too, who consoled us when we were hurt and punished us when we had it coming. Daddy was always there, a reassuring presence in his chair, with his tobacco can by his side, but there was no doubt that Mama was the strong one.

3

Over The Mountains to Georgia
in a Covered Wagon

After their marriage Mama and Daddy lived for a short time with Grandma Bolick (Bryson), but that didn't work out too well so they moved to a small house on Grandpa Ash's farm in Jackson County. Daddy worked the farm with Grandpa, and Mama's brothers, and earned just enough to support his wife and rapidly growing family. My sister, Ella Mae, was born in 1909 and my brother Hays in February 1912. Mama worked harder than ever, and soon realized that being married wasn't the end of the drudgery she had known when she was growing up, it had just been shifted from one place to another. But it was her own home now, and her own family, and if the realization of her girlhood dreams was something less than perfect, she was young and strong and surely things would get better for them.

But things didn't get better very fast. During the period 1910-1912, the country was going through an economic recession. There was a lot of unemployment and prices for farm products fell to a very low level. Grandpa Ash's farm just wasn't big enough to support all the children, single and married, that lived off of it. So Daddy started looking for some other way to make a living, and in 1911 he thought he had found it. One of his older brothers had moved to north Georgia, and he sent back word that there was big money to be made by planting cotton, and that large landowners were looking for sharecroppers. When

Daddy wrote back that he was interested, his brother helped him get on as a tenant with his landlord.

Daddy was very excited about all the money he was going to make, and the fact that he knew absolutely nothing about growing cotton didn't discourage him in the least. So in the early spring of 1912 he loaded Mama, Ella Mae, Hays, and all their household possessions in a covered wagon with their milk cow tied behind, hitched up his old mule to the wagon and set out over the mountains to Madison County, Georgia.

Hays was a newborn baby and Ella Mae was only two and a half years old, but she remembers that ride to Georgia in the wagon. It took four or five days to make the journey, and people in the farms along the way gave them food and water and let them camp for the night on their land. Maybe that's part of the reason that at age ninety my oldest sister still believes in the goodness of people as a whole, although even she has to admit that there are some bad apples in the barrel these days.

They finally arrived in Madison County and moved into their house on the Stewart farm. It wasn't much, that first place. Just a rough cabin on a few acres of land, which was all Daddy could work by himself. But it was a place of their own, even though they were only tenants, and for the first time in her life my Mama was out from under the thumb of an older woman. When she was growing up it was her Mama, who was a fair but stern taskmistress, and during the first year of her marriage to my father she found out that mothers-in-law are even harder to please than mothers.

I never knew my Grandma Bolick. She died in nineteen-twenty, four years before I was born. But my Mama told me a lot about her, and I formed a picture of a physically small woman who made up in willpower and

Over the mountains to Georgia

sheer determination for what she lacked in stature. Although her maiden name, George, was certainly not Irish, there must have been some Celtic blood on her mother's side. Mama described her as being red-headed and blue eyed , with a temper to match her hair. It's not surprising, then, that Mama was glad to finally be out on her own.

That first year was hard, and Daddy had to learn about growing cotton the hard way, by trial and error. He barely managed to harvest enough cotton to pay his debts to his landlord. The next year should have been better. Daddy had learned a lot about cotton, and conditions were right for a good crop. But then disaster struck - in the form of the boll weevil, that pesky insect imported from Mexico that attacked the cotton bolls and destroyed the developing cotton inside. Almost all of Daddy's crop was destroyed, and he went further in debt to the landlord, Mr. Stewart.

Then they got a break. World War I broke out in Europe, and the United States began to build up its Army against the possibility that it might be drawn into the conflict. A bigger Army meant more uniforms, which meant more cloth and more cotton to make it. The price of cotton rose dramatically and as luck would have it, conditions were all favorable for a bumper crop. When the harvest was in and all their debts were settled, they actually had a little left over.

But that was before Mama took over the reins, and Daddy was still handling the money. And although he didn't lose it gambling or drink it up, he did squander most of it on things they didn't really need, like a new coon dog, and a twelve gauge shotgun from the Sears, Roebuck catalog. He did buy some new clothes and shoes for the family, and candy and toys for the kids, but before the next Spring planting the money was all gone and he had to go back to the landlord for loans to put in his crops. That year the crop was not as good as the year before, and again he just barely realized enough from it to pay off his loans.

This pattern repeated itself over the next two years, and after the second year Daddy decided that he could do better somewhere else, and took a place in a neighboring county.

In nineteen-sixteen the United States entered the war. By that time Daddy had four children, so he wasn't drafted. Once again the price of cotton went up as thousands of new uniforms were needed, but Mama and Daddy didn't seem to be much better off. Their fifth child, J. C. (Jake), was born in nineteen-nineteen, ant they lost another child between Jake and me. I was born on June 18, 1924, on another farm outside the little town of Oglethorpe, Georgia, just a few months after my sister Ella Mae married Woody Lankford, the son of a neighboring farmer.

Ella Mae and Woody lived with us the first couple years of their marriage, and with Woody to help farm, along with Hays and Fred, who were big enough now to work in the fields, Daddy was able to take a bigger place and farm more acreage. So when I was a year old, just before Ella Mae gave birth to Willie Robert, we all moved to the Owens place in South Carolina.

4

A Hundred Pounds Is A Whole Lot Of Cotton

A lot of exciting things happened in nineteen-twenty-eight, the year that I was four years old, not the least of which was the birth of my baby brother, George Wallace.

I hadn't learned the facts of life yet, although you learn them pretty early on a farm. But I was old enough to notice that Mama's stomach had gotten awfully big and that she seemed to get tired more. One day she went to bed in the middle of the day and Daddy told me to go to Ella Mae's until he came for me. It seemed like I was there for a long time before he came and told me I had a new baby brother. I ran home to play with him, but he was too little, and all he did was sleep and cry. I decided that little brothers weren't much fun.

Mama and Daddy named him George Wallace, after the doctor who delivered him, Dr. George Wallace Parnell. This was fairly common in those days, to name a baby after the doctor, but I think Mama also did it out of sympathy for Doctor Parnell, who had recently lost his own sixteen year old son. He was killed in a tragic accident during a fight with another teenager at a High School basketball game. We called the baby Wallace, but he was called George when he went in the Navy during World War II and it's been George ever since.

I guess the thing I remember most vividly about nineteen-twenty-eight, though, is that Daddy let me pick

31

cotton that summer. The cotton crop was very good that year and it was important to get it picked as soon as possible after it ripened, since a heavy rain could beat it into the ground and damage it. So everyone who could pick was pressed into service, and although I really wasn't big enough to be of much help, Daddy let me think I was. He even agreed to pay me a dollar if I picked a hundred pounds. That sounded easy, and I was sure that I was going to make a lot of money.

Daddy had hired a couple of extra pickers, Negroes from another farm, and he paid them by the pound. Each picker had his own burlap ground sheet at one end of the field. When his picksack was full he emptied it onto his ground sheet, and at the end of the day the sheet was tied and weighed before dumping the cotton into a wagon.

When the wagon with its high stake bed was full, it was hitched to a mule and pulled into Fountain Inn to the cotton gin where it was ginned and baled. The owner of the gin took a percentage of the cotton and cottonseed for his work, and cotton brokers usually bought the cotton on the spot, eliminating the necessity of hauling the heavy bales back to the farm. Since I was the baby of the family (not counting Wallace), Daddy sometimes let me ride in the wagon with him to take the cotton to the gin. And if the price of cotton was good that year, there might be a penny for me for candy to eat on the way home.

It was fascinating to watch the cotton being ginned. The loaded wagon was pulled inside the gin and a big pipe was lowered town to the cotton from the ceiling. When the power was turned on the pipe sucked up the cotton like a big vacuum cleaner, and fed it into the machinery where the cottonseed was extracted and separated. Then the cleaned cotton was blown into a big press where it was compressed into five hundred pound bales and banded with metal straps.

Before the wagon was pulled inside the gin I had to get down and wait outside. The operators used to frighten little boys like me by telling us that the big pipes would suck us up with the cotton and crush us into the bale. I realized as I grew older that the suction wasn't really that powerful, but it was a good story and I believed it at the time. It served its purpose and kept little boys out of the operator's way.

In those days, before the invention of the mechanical cotton picker, picking cotton was one of the hottest, dirtiest, and most backbreaking jobs known to man.

Cottonstalks only grew about knee high to an average man, and when the bolls broke open and the cotton hung out, the only way to pick it was by bending over and pulling the cotton from each boll with your fingers. Picking was done during the hottest part of the summer, and the ripe bolls had a hard shell that wore the skin off the fingers until they became toughened with calluses. In addition, there were several kinds of biting or stinging insects that liked to hide under the leaves. One of the worst was a large green caterpillar with a brown saddle shaped mark on its back, giving it its name, "packsaddle". Its back was covered with sharp little spines like nettles, and when you touched them with your bare fingers they burned like fire. Since it's virtually impossible to pick cotton cleanly wearing even the thinnest of gloves, pickers were at the mercy of these creatures.

A hundred pounds of cotton doesn't sound like much if you say it real fast, but I found out the hard way that it took a whole lot of picking to get that hundred pounds. Mama had made me a picksack out of a flour sack, since I was too little to use the burlap bags the other pickers used, and the first morning I put the strap around my shoulder and started off down a row of cotton. I guess I didn't pick the stalks very clean, especially after my first encounter with a packsaddle, because Daddy or one of the other pickers always followed me to clean up what I left behind. When I reached the end of the row I was surprised to find that my picksack wasn't even half full, and it was almost mid-morning before I poured my first sackfull onto my own little groundsheet. But I kept going, with a few rest and water stops, until the noonday dinner break.

I was sure I had my hundred pounds, and wanted Daddy to weigh it But he said to wait until the end of the day. When the sun went down and the ground sheets were gathered up and tied for weighing, I waited impatiently as mine was put on the end of the big balance scales. Of course I couldn't read, but it seemed to me that the scale didn't move very much, and I could hardly believe my ears when Daddy said I had picked twenty pounds. I asked him how much more I needed and my heart sank when he said about four times that much.

It seemed like every muscle in my body hurt that night, but Mama made me soak in a washtub full of hot water, and next morning I was back in the cottonfields. I picked my hundred pounds of cotton by the end of the week, or at least Daddy gave me credit for that much. Maybe he put his hand on the end of the scales a little bit when he weighed me in, but he paid me off Saturday night with one hundred pennies in a tobacco sack with a draw string at the top. It was the first, and probably the hardest, money I ever earned.

5

Daddy's Model T

Cotton brought a good price in nineteen-twenty-eight, so there was a little money left over after Daddy paid off his loans. The boys got new overalls, Belle got material for a new dress, and Mama even made herself a new Sunday dress. That Christmas we had candy canes on the tree along with the homemade decorations of paper ornaments and popcorn strings. For the first time in my life I got a store-bought toy from Santa Claus, a wooden train engine, painted red, that was big enough for me to sit on and push myself around the house.

But the big news that fall was our first automobile! Daddy traded Mama's best milk cow and a hundred dollars for a secondhand Model T Ford Sedan. It was black, with four doors, a windshield and roof, and side curtains that buttoned up all around when it rained.

Mama had a fit when he told her he had traded her cow. Not only did the cow provide milk and butter for us, but Mama earned a little extra money by selling butter and buttermilk to the General Store in town. The one cow that she had left would give barely enough milk for our own family. I think that was about the time she decided that she would have to take over the financial reins of the family.

Daddy was proud as a peacock of his new possession, and kept it washed and shined until its black paint fairly glowed. Of course, he had never driven a car before, and his first attempts at learning to drive were hilarious as well as frightening. Once he drove it right through the back of the barn while hanging on for dear life and shouting, "Whoa, whoa!" at the top of his lungs.

But he finally learned, although he never was a very good driver. I remember watching him go through the routine of setting the throttle, advancing the spark, and then getting out and cranking the engine until it started with a cough and a bang, then chugged away as only a Model T could. I didn't get to ride in it very often, since we didn't have a lot of money for gasoline, but each time I did was a new and exciting adventure. We only had that car for about two years. Hays wrecked it beyond repair by running into a wagon full of cotton while he was learning to drive.

Hays also just about wrecked our happy home by trading Nell for a new shotgun.

Nell was our little dog. Or I should say she was Hays' dog, but in addition to being the best rat terrier in the county, she was the family pet. All farms in those days had corn cribs for storing ears of corn until they were needed for animal feed or to grind for corn meal. These cribs had floors set off the ground on two-by-fours, and screen wire sides so that the corn could dry out. Rats loved them, and used to live and breed under the floors, feeding on the corn at the bottom. Every fall, when the cribs were empty and before the new crop was stored in them, the farmers would tear up the floorboards and kill the rats.

Nell was a champion rat killer. She was a little thing, but fast as lightning. As soon as a board was pulled up and a rat ran out, she would pounce on it, grab it by the back of the neck, give it one bite of her jaws and drop it, dead. She

Daddy's Model T

had acquired quite a reputation in Greenville County, and Hays had a lot of offers to buy her but turned them all down. That winter, however, one of the neighbors made him an offer he couldn't refuse - an offer to trade him a new twelve gauge shotgun for Nell.

When he came home one day proudly showing off his new shotgun and told us he had traded Nell for it, the whole family practically went into shock. I cried and Belle cried, and the rest of the family would hardly speak to him. At first he was defensive, saying she was his dog and he could trade her if he wanted to. But after a couple days of the cold shoulder treatment and, I suspect, missing her himself, he returned the shotgun and got Nell back. He never thought of trading her again. She lived with us for the rest of her life, and died at a ripe old age after we moved away from the farm.

6

Sheriff Phillips and The Bootlegger

Nineteen-twenty-eight was also the year that I came face to face with violent death for the first time.

Our house sat at the end of a dirt road, about half a mile from a two lane county road. At the corner where our lane intersected the paved road there was a small country store with a gasoline pump, a "filling station", as we called it then. One night just after dark Hays came running down the lane yelling that the Sheriff had shot a bootlegger at the filling station. Daddy quickly cranked up the Model T and Hays and Fred and Jake and I piled in. I don't think Daddy realized that I was along until after we pulled up at the station, but by that time I had already seen the body. It was lying on the oil soaked dirt next to the gasoline pump, just behind the open trunk of an old car, and had been partially covered by an old piece of canvas. There was a small puddle of something dark near the covered head, and I could see by the arm that was sticking out from under the canvas that he was a colored man.

By this time a small crowd of men and boys had gathered around the station, and the owner, Mr. James Abernathy, was telling everybody what had happened. He took his time and spared none of the gory details. This was probably the most exciting thing he had ever witnessed, and he was going to enjoy it to the fullest.

According to Mr. Abernathy, Sheriff Phillips was in the filling station drinking a Coca Cola, with his police car parked around back, when the Negro pulled up to the gas pump. Since it was unusual to see a black man driving a car in those days, the Sheriff walked up to him and asked him who the car belonged to. When he said it belonged to him, the Sheriff told him to get out of the car and open the trunk. He did, and then, the Sheriff said, as the Negro opened the trunk he reached for a gun inside it. That's when Sheriff Phillips shot him twice in the back. Then he looked in the trunk and saw that it was full of half gallon jars of corn whiskey. Mr. Abernathy came out of the station and saw the whiskey before the Sheriff loaded it into his police car and took it away for evidence. He didn't see any gun, but he guessed the Sheriff took that away for evidence, too.

The people in the crowd stood around talking about the shooting until a hearse from the colored funeral home in Fountain Inn pulled up and took the body away. Then they slowly dispersed and went back to their homes.

Things being the way they were in South Carolina in those days, the death of one Negro didn't attract much attention in the rest of the county. There was a bare two or three line mention of it in the next week's Fountain Inn paper, including the fact that the Coroner had ruler it, "justifiable homicide".

But it made an impression on me, and I never forgot how that body looked, or the way the people in that crowd treated it as if it were just another piece of trash.

7

The Crash of '29

For the Bolick family, the Great Depression of the Nineteen Thirties began in the Fall of nineteen-twenty-nine.

After the good crop and high cotton prices the year before, Daddy decided to make some real money in nineteen-twenty-nine. He persuaded Judge Owens to give him another fifty acres, now that Hays and Fred and Jake were big enough to do a full days work in the fields. Along with Woody's land, they planted about two hundred acres. A few acres were put into corn and alfalfa to feed the stock and hogs, but mostly they planted the money crop, cotton.

The weather cooperated that year, with plenty of sunshine and just enough rain, and by July the fields were white with cotton bursting from its bolls. It was a bumper crop, ready for picking. I didn't help pick it that year. I guess Daddy figured I would just be in the way, and besides, I was big enough now to help Mama and Belle with the chickens and hogs and with the kitchen garden. While I wouldn't admit it, I was relieved that I didn't have to go back into the fields and face the packsaddles again. I worked pretty hard that summer, just the same, carrying water to the kitchen, feeding the chickens, slopping the hogs, and hoeing and weeding the yellow corn and beans and tomatoes in the garden. Belle also taught me how to milk our old cow, Bessy, although I was still too young to be trusted with doing that chore by myself.

There was an overwhelming feeling of optimism in the air that year. The crops were good, the weather perfect for picking, and cotton prices the highest they had been in years. Daddy had only a second grade education, so he didn't know much about the economy, but he knew good news when he heard it. And everything he heard was good. A lot of the landowners were holding back their cotton, not selling it to the brokers at the gin, but keeping it for later sale at what they expected would be higher prices.

Judge Owens was one of those who held back, and Daddy decided to follow his lead. When our cotton was ginned Daddy sold just enough of his share to pay for the ginning, and to pay off his advances from the Judge. The rest of it was hauled back to our farm and stored in the barn, and when the barn was full the rest was piled in the yard.

It was a good plan, except that it didn't work. On October 29, 1929, the stock market crashed and the price of cotton fell through the floor. It went from fifty cents a pound to twenty-five cents and then to ten cents in a matter of hours. Before anyone could react, the brokers quit buying it at any price. Some of the farmers still had cotton in their barns which hadn't been ginned, and when they took it to the gin they were told that they would have to pay cash for the ginning. The operators wouldn't gin it for a percentage of the yield.

It was a disaster for our family, and wiped out everything we had made the year before. Judge Owens let us and Ella Mae and Woody stay on in our houses through the winter, but he wouldn't advance any more money, and let Daddy know that he didn't intend to plant cotton the next spring, so we would have to find another place to live by then. That was a pretty lean winter, although we had enough to eat and enough firewood to keep us warm. Daddy butchered our last two hogs for meat, and Mama killed some of her chickens, keeping her best laying hens for eggs. We still had corn in the crib for corn meal, and old Bessy for milk and Mama's canned goods under the house, so we didn't go hungry. We ate a lot of cornbread and milk that winter, and I still love it to this day. Mama and Belle sewed, making clothes out of whatever material that was available, including flour sacks that came in printed patterns just for that purpose. Daddy and Woody spent a lot of time going around the county trying to find us a place to move to the next spring.

Two of Mama's younger brothers were living at Lowell, North Carolina, and working in the textile mills there. Since there wasn't going to be any work for them on the farm the next year, Hays and Fred decided to go up there and try to find work in the mills. The recession that followed the stock market crash hadn't yet become a real depression, so some of the mills were still running, and there was some part-time work to be had. So they packed their things and went to live with their Uncle Bill in Lowell. He helped them get on at the mill where he worked, and for the first time in their lives they were drawing a salary each week, even though it was only a few dollars.

Daddy and Woody's efforts finally paid off, too, and early in March of nineteen-thirty they both found places, although not on the same farm. Ours was a small house, about two miles closer to town than the Owens place, on a farm owned by a Mr. Williams. He wasn't planting cotton that year either, but he gave us free rent and a few acres for planting corn and vegetables, in exchange for looking after the place and planting corn and alfalfa for his stock. Woody got a similar deal from old Doctor White, just about a mile down the road. The first of April the men loaded our household furnishings onto the wagons, hitched up the mules, and moved us to our new homes.

Our new house wasn't much different than the last one, only smaller. But our family was smaller now too, at least for the moment, and this house was located on a two lane county road so that it was almost like living in town. I thought Ella Mae's house was more interesting. It sat on the side of a hill that sloped down to a ravine that was all covered with morning glory and some kind of spreading vine. There was also a woods at the bottom of the hill with a wide creek running through it, and Bob and I spent a lot of hours exploring these new surroundings.

8

Our Last Year on the Farm

In nineteen-thirty I started school and my whole family, except Daddy and me, got the flu.

When we lived on the Owens' place, Belle and Jake had to walk about half a mile to the main road to get their school bus. Here in our new place we were right on the county road and the bus stopped just a few hundred yards from our house. I was a little bit disappointed, as I had been looking forward to walking with them to the bus stop, but I was so excited about starting to school that I got over it very quickly.

At that time in South Carolina children were only required to go to school until they were fourteen, or had completed the sixth grade, whichever came first. Since farm children were often taken out of school for as much as a month of the school year to help with the planting or harvest, it was difficult for some of them to complete the school work necessary for promotion to the next grade each year, and many of them got discouraged and lost interest. I think that had happened to Belle. She was almost fourteen in September of nineteen-thirty, and seemed to be looking forward to the day when she could quit. Jake, too, talked about getting a job and making money as soon as he was old enough.

If I sensed my brother and sister's lack of enthusiasm on that first day of school, I didn't let it dampen my spirits in the least. With the one exception of my brief stint at picking cotton, I hadn't had to work in the fields yet, and school seemed like a new and exciting experience. Although it didn't prove to be quite as perfect as I imagined it would be, I did like it, and did very well that first year. However, just when I was beginning to really get into it, the family came down with the flu and I had to stay home to help take care of them.

Around the end of the nineteenth century, influenza epidemics killed thousands of people every few years. By the nineteen thirties the flu wasn't quite so deadly, as more medicines had been developed to fight it, but there still were no wonder drugs such as sulfa or penicillin. It was still a serious disease, and one that was highly contagious. Belle got it first, probably from exposure to it at school, and it quickly spread through the rest of the family, missing only Daddy and me. Mama was about six months pregnant with my sister Dot at the time, and when she came down with the flu everyone was worried that she might lose the baby.

It took about two weeks for the disease to run its course, and there wasn't much anyone could do except keep the patients warm and give them plenty of liquids, along with the vile tasting medicine provided by Doctor Parnell. Daddy and I did the best we could, and by the time Jake, who was the last to get it, came down with it Belle was almost well and was able to help us. We got through it somehow without Mama losing the baby.

I missed almost a month of school, but so did about half the rest of the kids, and with a lot of extra homework we were able to catch up. We still didn't have electricity in our house and I spent long hours doing homework by lamplight at the kitchen table.

We had another austere Christmas that year, with no toys or presents for any of us. But we had a tree with candles and homemade decorations of strings of popcorn.

Daddy managed to get a bag of peppermint candy sticks for us, and Mama killed and roasted a big fat hen for Christmas Dinner. As bad as things were, we were probably better off than a lot of families in the country, which was beginning to become mired deep in the depression. Everyone blamed it on our Republican president, Mr. Herbert Hoover, but it actually was a world-wide condition and there was little that he or anyone else could do about it.

My youngest sister, Dorothy Lou, was born at home on February 3rd, 1931, my oldest brother Hays' birthday. When she was about a month old Mama and Daddy decided to move us to Lowell, North Carolina. Hays and Fred were working in the mill there, and they managed to find a job for Daddy as a porter and sweeper. They were also able to get us a company house in a section of town called Oakland. So early in March Daddy hired a truck to move our possessions to our new home.

As the oldest boy still at home, Jake was given the responsibility of helping to load the truck and ride with the driver to Lowell. Since our household goods didn't fill the whole truck, a piece of canvas was hung from the ceiling near the rear and our cow, old Bessy, was loaded in and the tail gate closed. Jake and the driver pulled out, with the rest of the family to follow in a car that Hays had managed to borrow from a friend in Oakland. About ten miles down the road the right rear wheel came off the truck, throwing open the tailgate and tossing poor old Bessy out into a ditch. Jake said she took off at full speed across a field and it took him the better part of an hour to catch her.

The truck driver had to walk three miles to the nearest telephone to call his office, and it was three or four hours before a repair truck came out to fix the wheel. They arrived at the house in Oakland after dark that evening, having taken all day to cover the fifty miles from Fountain Inn.

I wasn't with them, as I didn't move to Lowell when the rest of the family did. Since I only had three months left to finish the First Grade at Fountain Inn, I stayed with Ella Mae and Woody until school was out. By that time Woody had also found a job with one of the mills in Lowell, and when they moved into a house just behind ours in Oakland, I came with them to rejoin my family.

Part Two

Growing Up In A Mill Town

During The Depression

9

Oakland, North Carolina

Like the houses in the other mill villages in and around Lowell, all the houses in Oakland were built pretty much on the same plan; a rectangular shaped one-story wooden box, with two bedrooms, a living room which often served as a third bedroom, a kitchen big enough for cooking and eating, and a bathroom with a toilet, washbasin, and a big cast iron bathtub. Small fireplaces in each room, with grates for burning coal or wood, provided heat in the winter months. Our house also had a front porch with four steps, where I used to sit and wait for Daddy and my older brothers to come home from the mill.

For the first time in my life I lived in a house with running water and electricity. Of course, the electric lights consisted of bare bulbs in sockets hanging down from the ceiling in each room, but they provided much more light than kerosene lamps, and I spent hours reading at the kitchen table or curled up in front of a fireplace. The running water came from a big water tank that stood on its steel legs high above the village. It was cold water, and we had no hot water heater, but in the summer time it was almost lukewarm and we could take a bath in it. In the winter we added a couple gallons of steaming hot water from the reservoir on Mama's cook stove to the tap water for our weekly baths.

We only lived in Oakland for about a year, but during that time my two oldest brothers, Hays and Fred, got married. Hays married a girl named Irene and they moved into a company house on Stowe Street in Art Cloth. Fred got a girl named Pauline pregnant, and married her and moved in with her and her Mama in a house in Oakland. Pauline wasn't a very good wife, and a worse mother. The baby died when it was eight months old, mostly from neglect my Mama said, and Fred left her. She had him arrested for non-support, and I went with Mama to see him in the county jail in Gastonia. It was the first time I had ever seen anyone in jail. When he got out he took off for another part of the State and we didn't hear from him for several months.

My brother Fred was born about thirty years too soon. If he had been born in the forties or fifties, he might have become a Country Western music star. He was a handsome young man, with a very outgoing personality and a good singing voice.

Just after moving to North Carolina, he acquired an old Gibson guitar and learned to play it. When Pauline divorced him so that she could marry the father of her latest child, he returned to Lowell and went back to work in the mill. But music was his first love, and he played and sang anywhere that he could get people to listen. Billing himself as "Fred Bolick, The Singing Cowboy," he persuaded the Gastonia radio station to give him a fifteen minute spot at six a.m., three days a week. Of course he didn't get paid for it, but the important thing was that he was being heard and becoming known around the county. And he was sure that he would be discovered by a record company or offered a paying spot by one of the Charlotte stations.

Things didn't quite work out that way, and after five years and two more wives, he joined the Army and had reached the rank of Sergeant when World II broke out.

When I think about living in Oakland, one of the things I remember best is Mama's potato soup. Nearly every day she made a big pot of potato soup, which contained potatoes and onions and corn meal. She would put the pot on the stove after breakfast in the morning and cook it slowly for several hours. After serving it at the noon meal she would set what was left on the back of the stove, to be reheated at suppertime. By the time I got home from school it would be cold, but I would help myself to a bowl of it anyway. I learned to love cold potato soup, and it was many years before I realized that I had been eating vichyssoise and didn't know it.

10

Lowell and Art Cloth

In the nineteen-thirties, Lowell, North Carolina was a town with a population of less than one thousand people, about eighty percent of whom worked in the mills. The other twenty percent was made up of tradesmen, county employees, teachers, and an ever increasing number of unemployed. It wasn't so much a town as a collection of mill villages made up of the small houses that surrounded each mill. These houses were owned by the mill operators and rented to the workers at a very nominal rent. Each of the villages had an official name at the Post Office, but they were usually referred to by the name of the mill that owned them. So Woodlawn, where I spent most of my formative years, was better known as, "Art Cloth".

The center of Lowell was built around the intersection of two roads; a county road that ran parallel to the Southern Railway tracks, and a local road that dead-ended into it. Art Cloth was on this local road, half a mile east of the intersection and just across the P & N (Piedmont & Northern) Railroad tracks. The business district of Lowell consisted of a Post Office, barber shop, general store, and a drug store with a soda fountain, which was the social center for the young people of the community. The town's two doctors, Dr. Reed and Dr. Grove, had second floor offices above the drug store. Just west of the center of town,

Lowell High School was located on one side of the Southern Railroad tracks, and a boarding house for single schoolteachers, dubbed appropriately enough, "The Teacherage" by the townspeople, sat within easy walking distance of the high school on the other side. There were also two elementary schools, one near the high school and the other at Art Cloth.

Uncle Bill, and Grandma and Grandpa Ash, lived at Art Cloth, and Daddy worked in the Art Cloth mill, so when a company house came open there, we moved into it.

Art Cloth had only four streets and this first house was on Main Street, at the opposite end of the street from Gilliam's Grocery and Branch Post Office, Red's Barber Shop, and the combination Drug Store and Pool Hall. When we lived in Oakland I went to the Art Cloth Elementary School. It was only a half mile, if you cut through the woods and across the P&N tracks as I did, but it seemed longer than that. So I was real glad to see that our house on Main Street was only a few blocks from the school, and I could even come home for lunch.

11

The Red Brick Schoolhouse

The Art Cloth Elementary School was a red brick building right in the middle of the village, at the intersection of Main Street and Linebarger Street. It sat on a slight hill overlooking this intersection, with the Principal's house next door to it, and served the people of the village as a community center. First, of course, it was a school, with six classrooms for seven grades, and an auditorium that seated about a hundred people. But it was also a place of worship, and a community theater for traveling road shows and silent movies.

The Woodlawn First Baptist Church held its services there on Sundays and on Wednesday evenings, and that's where I went to Sunday School until I was in High School. Traveling magicians, hypnotists, animal trainers, and starving vaudevillians put on free performances in the auditorium from time to time, trusting to the audience to deposit a few coins when they passed the hat. But the thing we looked forward to the most was the movies,

About once a month a movie operator would come to town and put up his posters on the streetlight poles, advertising a motion picture show to be shown in the school auditorium on Friday or Saturday night. The program usually consisted of a comedy such as Laurel and Hardy or Buster Keaton, and a Western feature. The movies had names, but we knew them only by their

58

The Red Brick Schoolhouse

cowboy stars - Buck Jones, Tom Mix, Johnny Mack Brown, Hoot Gibson, etc. Of course these were silent movies, but the operator brought along an assistant who played the piano to heighten the drama of the film. Quite often the music was out of sync with the action, bringing boos and catcalls from the audience which only added to the enjoyment of the program. Admission to the movie was ten cents, and we boys sometimes earned free passes by putting up the advertising posters.

The Elementary School itself had grades one through seven. There were no kindergartens in most North Carolina school systems in those days. The first five grades had their own home rooms, and the sixth and seventh grades, which were taught by the Principal, Mr. Helton, were in the same room. On the surface this would seem to be very confusing, but it actually worked out quite well. While one grade was being taught one subject, the other grade was working on their last assignment. When I reached the exalted status of a sixth grader I found that I quickly adapted to the arrangement, and could tune out Mr. Helton as he was teaching the other class.

Of course, in nineteen-thirty-two I was only in the third grade. I still liked school, especially reading, and devoured any books or magazines that I could get my hands on. My third grade teacher, Miss Grace Cloninger, recognized my interest and encouraged me by giving me things to read and discussing the things I read with me. She even went so far as to talk to my mother about the possibility of adopting me, promising to see that I went to college and got a good education. But Mama thanked her and declined her offer.

12

Running Away To Texas

My voracious appetite for reading got me in trouble when I was in the third grade. Some of the most popular periodicals in those days were what were called "Pulp Magazines," deriving their name from the cheap paper they were printed on. These magazines had such names as "Western Stories," "Mystery Magazine," "True Adventures," "Flying Aces," and of course, "True Love Stories" and "True Romances" for the ladies. While I read any that I could lay my hands on, even the love stories if that was all I could find, my favorites were stories about flying, and the western magazines with their cowboy stories. I could lose myself for hours in stories about Captain Eddie Rickenbacker and the Red Baron, or about cowboys riding, roping, branding cattle and fighting off rustlers. In my mind's eye I was right there with them.

The locale for most of these tales of the Old West was Texas, and I began to daydream of running away from home and going to Texas to become a Cowboy. Just southeast of Gastonia, our County Seat, and about ten miles from Lowell, was a little town called Dallas. I had never been to Dallas, but just from the name I was sure it was in Texas, and if I went there I could be a Cowboy. Of course I would have to run away, because my Mama would never let me go if she knew about it. So I began to make plans for running away from home. Not because I was unhappy or mistreated at home, but just so I could become a Cowboy.

I guess it was the new boots that caused me to act on my fantasies. All of the kids my age went barefoot in the summer time, or wore old worn-out tennis shoes that were coming apart at the seams. But when school started we got new shoes if our parents could afford them, and this year I got a pair of high-topped shoes that became cowboy boots in my imagination. They weren't actually new, but were a pair that my brother Jake had outgrown and Mama had put away and saved until I grew into them. But they were new to me, and now I was all set to go to Texas and ride the bucking broncos. The next morning I would leave for school as usual, but instead of going to school I would keep on going down the P&N Railroad tracks until I got to Dallas.

Once I made up my mind I was so full of excitement that I just had to tell somebody. I couldn't tell my little brother Wallace, because he couldn't keep a secret, and would run right to Mama and tell her. So I decided to tell Jack Eppley. Jack's family lived next door to us, and he was my best friend. He liked Cowboys, too, and we played Cowboys and Indians together a lot, although he liked Cops and Robbers best and John Dillinger was his favorite. The night before I was going to leave home I told him about it and asked him if he wanted to go with me. He said he'd like to, but he didn't have any boots so he guessed he'd better not go. I didn't try to talk him into it, but made him cross his heart and hope to die that he wouldn't tell anybody where I had gone.

The next morning I started out to school with Jack as usual, but before we got there I cut through the woods to the P&N tracks and started out toward Dallas. At first I skipped along the tracks, stepping on each crosstie and trotting my imaginary horse. Outlaws ambushed me at a turn in the trail, but I pulled out my two pearl handled Colt 44's and shot and killed all ten of them. My pinto pony

63

shied at a rattle (garter) snake and almost threw me, but I pulled on the reins and got her under control and went galloping on across the prairie,

It was a warm September day and along toward mid morning I began to get pretty hot and thirsty. There was a little creek just down below the tracks, so I slid down the bank and got down on my hands and knees and drank Indian fashion. The water probably wasn't very clean, what with all the mills in the vicinity, but it tasted good to me. The drink made me hungry and I took my lunch out of my pocket and ate the peanut butter sandwich Mama had made for me when I told her I had to stay at school during the lunch period to work on something for my teacher. The combination of the sun and the food made me sleepy, so I sat on the ground with my back against a tree and took a nap.

When I woke up I didn't know what time it was, but it seemed to me that the sun which had been almost overhead was now lower in the sky toward Gastonia, so I guessed I had slept for quite a while. I got up and started to walk down the tracks again, but it was pretty hot and I began to sweat, and Jake's old shoes didn't fit very well and were beginning to wear a blister on one of my heels. My pace slowed as my enthusiasm for going to Texas began to wear off. How far was it to Dallas, anyway? It seemed like I had been walking forever and I still hadn't seen a horse or a cowboy or even a jackrabbit, just the same old North Carolina red clay on both sides of the railroad tracks.

I figured it was probably about time for school to let out, and I began to wonder what my Mama would think when I didn't come home with the other kids. She'd probably be mad at first, and then she'd start to worry about me. I didn't want her to worry, and I sure didn't want her to get mad enough to use that hickory switch she kept behind the kitchen door. Maybe I should just go on back home and wait 'til I was a little bigger to go to Texas. Suiting actions to the thought, I sat down on one of the metal rails and took off my shoes. Then tying the laces together, I threw them across my shoulder and started back the way I had come.

As it turned out Mama wasn't really worried, although she was pretty mad at me. When I didn't come home from school she went next door to the Eppley's house and she and Mrs. Eppley sat Jack down and made him tell them where I was. Knowing that I couldn't get into too much trouble on the P&N tracks, since the only two daily trains between Gastonia and Charlotte had already come and gone, she decided to just wait and let me come home when I got good and tired.

I dragged into the house about supper time, expecting the worst. But Mama didn't get the hickory switch, just told me to wash up for supper. She didn't ask me where I'd been or anything, but the cold shoulder she gave me hurt worse than if she'd given me a whipping. And the smirks on the faces of my brothers made me feel like crawling under the table and hiding. I took a lot of kidding about going to Texas from the other kids the next day at school, for Jack Eppley had to go and blab it to everybody. I decided that the next time I ran away from home, if there ever was a next time, I sure wouldn't tell him about it.

13

A Very Special Christmas

The year nineteen-thirty-three was the low point of the Depression for the Bolick family. Just about all the mills in the Country were closed, and President Roosevelt's NRA public assistance programs had not begun to take effect. So unemployment was at an all time high. Daddy and my brother Jake managed to get a day or two now and then on the WPA, but that barely brought in enough money to keep food on the table. Belle had gotten married the year after we moved to North Carolina, and luckily her husband, Walt Cook, was still getting two or three days work a week in the only mill in our part of the country that was still running. He and Belle and their baby boy, Henry, moved in with us, and with his weekly paycheck added to the pot we didn't go hungry. But there wasn't anything left over for non-essentials.

Christmas that year promised to be pretty bleak. I had really had my heart set on an air rifle, so that I could go down by the river and shoot at rabbits and birds and squirrels, and pretend they were outlaws. But I couldn't see any way that I was going to get one. I no longer believed in Santa Claus. The brutal realities of the Depression had forced parents to dispel that myth, along with the Easter Bunny and the Tooth Fairy, and I knew that Mama and Daddy didn't have any money for Christmas presents. But I still couldn't quite give up hope, and when I went to bed on Christmas Eve I said a little prayer that maybe all the grown-ups might be wrong, and that there might really be a Santa Claus.

Somebody up there answered my prayer. Of course I knew that it wasn't Santa Claus, but my sister Belle, who left that shiny new single shot lever action Daisy Air Rifle under the Christmas Tree, along with two round cardboard tubes of BB shot. I was so excited that I didn't stop to wonder how she was able to afford to buy it for me, and it wasn't until I was a few years older that I realized how she must have scraped and saved and deprived herself to get that extra dollar she spent to keep me from being disappointed on Christmas morning.

By the middle of the next year the country was beginning to dig itself out from the worst of the Great Depression, and by Christmas of nineteen-thirty-four some of the mills were running again, at least on a part time basis. Both Daddy and Jake were working a few days a week, and Mama had taken in a couple boarders to supplement the family income. For Christmas that year Wallace and I got our first bicycle, a used one that we shared, which Mama bought for five dollars. It was a good Christmas, and I was very excited about the bicycle, but no Christmas could ever be as wonderful as the one when I got the air rifle.

Contrary to my great expectations, I didn't decimate the small animal population around our house. I found that the birds were very hard to hit, and when I did hit a rabbit or a squirrel I only stung them a little bit and they ran off before I could reload and get off another shot. I ended up using the air rifle mostly for target practice, shooting at knots on tree limbs and pinging tin cans. Once I succumbed to an irresistible urge and shot out the bulb in the street light in front of our house, which resulted in my getting a stern lecture from our local Deputy Sheriff, several lashes with Mama's hickory switch, and the loss of the air rifle for a month. After that I confined myself to target shooting and to using the empty rifle for playing Cowboys and Indians.

Christmas 1933

14

Summer At Grandpa's

The year that I was ten I spent the summer with Grandma and Grandpa Ash.

When most of the mills shut down Grandpa had left Art Cloth and rented a small farm near Belmont, about five miles from Lowell. The house that he had had on Black Street in Art Cloth was bigger than the one we lived in on Main Street, so we moved into it. It was built on a lot that sloped away steeply from front to back, and Daddy did some excavating and built two extra bedrooms on the lower level. This gave us five bedrooms and made room for Mama to take in some more boarders. We also had a much bigger lot, with almost a half acre of land for Daddy to plant his garden.

On his rented acres Grandpa raised hogs, milked three cows, and grew corn and alfalfa to feed them and the two mules that came with the farm. He paid the rent to the owner out of what he earned on the farm. He fed and butchered the hogs and sold the meat, and milked the cows. Grandma churned the butter and sold it and the buttermilk, so they made out pretty well even during the worst of the depression. I now look back on the time spent with Grandma and Grandpa that summer as some of the best days of my life, although there were a few times during my stay with them when I wouldn't have said that.

Grandpa would have been in his late sixties then, and Grandma a few years younger. Although people like them didn't make much fuss about wedding anniversaries in those days, they had been married for about fifty years and had raised eight children. In spite of the absence of any outward signs of affection between them, they were very devoted to each other, and I doubt that they had spent more than a dozen nights apart in those fifty years, and then only in extreme cases of sickness in the family. Their given names were Coleman and Callie, and while she always called him "Cole", I never heard him call her anything but "Ma" or "your Gran'ma".

Grandpa Ash may have had his own religious beliefs, but if so he kept them to himself. The only times I ever knew him to set foot inside a church was for a wedding or a funeral. Grandma, on the other hand, was very religious. She was a member of the Church of God, which was very strict in its doctrines and dictates, and while she didn't try to impose her beliefs on anyone else, she lived her religion every day and never missed church on Sunday, unless she was too ill to get there. One would have thought that she and Grandpa might have had some quarrels over their different views of religion, but that wasn't the case. They respected each other's convictions, and every Sunday Grandpa hitched up one of the mules to the buggy and drove Grandma to church, and picked her up when the service was over.

While I was with them I had to choose between going to church with Grandma, or staying home with Grandpa. At first I went with Grandma. But the services were long and loud and full of fire and brimstone, and the wooden seats were so hard that it was difficult for a ten-year old boy to sit still through them. So after a couple of times I found some excuse for staying with Grandpa.

Grandpa had been a big man when he was younger, and even with his shoulders stooped from age and hard work he was still over six feet tall. And I soon found out that he could still put in a full day's work. When I arrived at the farm the corn was just big enough for thinning, and that was the first thing he taught me. Corn was planted with a planter that was pulled by a mule. It dispensed the grains of corn into a prepared furrow, and to make sure of getting a good stand the planter was always set to sow more seeds that were actually needed. When the corn came up it had to be thinned out, cutting out the small seedlings and giving the bigger ones more room to grow. This didn't sound too difficult, but it proved to be rather tricky and very backbreaking work.

The thinning hoes were sharpened to a razor-like edge, and Grandpa showed me how to walk along a row and pluck out the smaller seedlings with the sharp corner of the hoe, leaving the remaining ones just about a foot apart. It was harder than it looked, and my first efforts resulted in my cutting down all the seedlings for two or three feet, and leaving clumps of them for the next two or three. But Grandpa was very patient with his instructions, and I soon began to do a passable job, although I was much slower at it than he was. He thinned two rows at a time, walking between them, while I did only one. His hoe would just seem to flick over the little corn stalks and they would be thinned out without him even slowing down. Before I reached the end of my one row he had finished his two and was meeting me halfway up the next two.

Luckily for me Grandpa took pity on me and knocked off early that first day. It felt like every muscle in my body was aching, some that I didn't even know I had. That night, after a good supper of ham and butter beans, and thick corn bread that she cooked in a Dutch Oven covered with coals in the fireplace, Grandma rubbed my aching muscles with lineament. I soon fell asleep and slept like a log until Grandpa woke me up just after daylight the next morning, to help him with the early morning chores.

During the next few weeks I learned a lot about the farm and about farming, and in some cases re-learned what I once knew but had forgotten. In addition to thinning corn I learned how to milk a cow again, plow a rather shaky furrow behind one of the old mules, slop the hogs and feed the other animals, pull one end of a crosscut saw, help Grandma churn the milk, and to ride the mules bareback. I learned enough, in fact, to decide that I never wanted to be a farmer.

But it wasn't all hard work, and even that became more enjoyable as I got more familiar with it and better at it. Grandma's cooking was wonderful, and my skinny frame began to fill out noticeably. And I especially enjoyed the quiet time in the evenings between supper and bedtime. With no electricity, they didn't have a radio. Grandpa didn't like them anyway, and said the best thing about a radio was the knob that turned it off, so we just sat in front of the big fireplace as the cooking coals died down, and talked about what we had done that day. Grandma read her Bible and I would sometimes read a book by the light of the kerosene lamp on the kitchen table until I got sleepy and crawled into the bed with the feather mattress in my little bedroom.

One of the things that I enjoyed most was riding the mules. There was a black one and a gray one, and they were used separately or as a team to do the plowing and cultivating, or to pull the farm wagons and the buggy, and do all the other heavy work around the farm. Sometimes they also served as riding horses for a ten-year old boy, but they didn't care much for that. Sunday on the farm was a day of rest, for both people and animals. Grandpa only did the essential things, like milking the cows and feeding the animals, and the mules seemed to have an internal seven day clock that told them when it was Sunday.

So they didn't take it kindly when I put a bridle on one of them and led him out of the barn and climbed on his back.

Grandpa didn't have a saddle, so I just put an old horse blanket across his back and climbed on. That wasn't easy to do, since he was so much bigger than I was, and not the least bit anxious to help me. But I devised a way of leading the mule alongside the rail fence of the barnyard and climbing up on the fence to mount. That was just the beginning of my problem, however, as the mule didn't want to leave the barn and I would have to kick him in the ribs with my bare feet every step of the way down the lane away from the house. But that all changed when I had gone as far as I wanted to go and turned his head back toward the barn. Then there was no holding him back, and it was all I could do to stay on his back by holding onto his mane, as he almost galloped back to his Sunday place of rest.

It didn't take long for the daily work routine to strengthen and harden my muscles, and by the time of Grandpa's Birthday Dinner late in the month I was as tough as nails. This birthday dinner was an annual event, on the Sunday closest to his birthday, and it was quite an affair. All of his children that could possibly make it were there, along with their wives and husbands and dozens of grandchildren and great-grandchildren. And as he got older, great-great-grandchildren.

The men would erect a table twenty or thirty feet long out of saw horses and planks, which the women would cover with white sheets for tablecloths. Every family that arrived brought food and put it on the table. There would

be ham, roast beef, chicken and dumplings, and a dozen
batches of fried chicken, all cooked North Carolina style
with a soft crust, but each batch just different enough to be
easily identifiable as to its creator, at least by the other
cooks. There were green beans and potato salad and fried
okra and candied sweet potatoes and mashed potatoes and
corn and peas and tomatoes, and every other kind of
vegetable imaginable, along with several batches of
cornbread and plate after plate of biscuits. And all kinds of
desserts; blackberry and peach cobblers, apple and peach
and pecan pies, cakes, and of course, my favorite of all –
banana pudding.

At either end of the long table a new ten gallon wash
tub, bought just for the occasion, was full of iced tea with a
ten pound chunk of ice floating in it. And off to one side
under the shade of a tree, we boys took turns cranking the
handle of a two-gallon ice cream freezer filled to the brim
with rich cream and strawberries or peaches or bananas.
As the ice cream froze it expanded and some of it would
escape from around the lid where it picked up a little of the
salt used on the ice for freezing, and was immediately
wiped off by the fingers of the younger children. Very few
things in life ever tasted as good as that salt flavored ice
cream.

After one of the Preachers said the blessing (we had
quite a few of them in the family) we would all dig in, each
family using their own plates and utensils that they had
brought with them, and for a while the only sound around
the table was the praising of this dish or that one and the
smacking of lips showing the crowd's appreciation of the
cooks' work. When everyone had gorged themselves, the
grown-ups would find a chair or a soft spot on the ground
under the trees where they would catch up on the news
from each other, or just close their eyes and take a nap,

while the children worked off their dinner by playing games or just horsing around.

One of my cousins, who was a couple years older than I was, got a little rough with me as we wrestled on the grass. Always in the past he had been able to get the best of me rather easily, but working on the farm had made me more than a match for him and this time I threw him down and pinned him. This made him mad and he charged at me again and I threw him again. When he got up, he took a swing at me and we started punching each other. Things might have gotten out of hand if one of our uncles hadn't pulled us apart and told us to cool off. After we calmed down we shook hands, and I couldn't help feeling a little bit proud when he rather grudgingly remarked that working with Grandpa must have been good for me.

When everybody started to leave Mama asked me if I wanted to come home with them, but I decided to stay on with Grandpa and Grandma until school started. Grandpa died while I was overseas in World War II, and I was always thankful for the memory of that one summer with him.

15

Mama's Boarding House

By the summer of nineteen-thirty-five the country was showing some signs of beginning to emerge from the worst of the Depression. Some of the mills in North and South Carolina were running again, and the mill at Art Cloth was running one shift five days a week and a second shift two or three days. But in order to get work, many mill workers were still forced to lead a nomadic life, going from one town to another, wherever work was available. Most of them were married and had families in Rock Hill or Shelby or Spartanburg, or some other town in the mill district, so when they got a job at a mill too far from home to commute every day, they had to have a place to live from Monday to Friday. And, of course, there were some single men and women workers who needed a full time residence.

The year that we moved into the bigger house on Black Street my brother Jake got married and moved to Burlington, North Carolina to work in the mill there, and Belle and Walt moved out into a house of their own. That left only Mama, Daddy, Wallace and Dot and me at home, so Mama now had extra rooms for boarders. She had no trouble getting them, as she kept a clean house and set a table with plentiful quantities of good food. Among her first boarders were two young ladies, Eudora Hyatt and Alexandria Shaw, who stayed with us for several years. And there was Johnny Matthews, a bachelor in his mid twenties, who lived with us so long that he almost became part of the family.

Word of Mama's boarding house soon got around, and before long she had a waiting list. In order to accommodate two more, Wallace and I had to give up our room and each of us move into a room with two of the men boarders. This wasn't quite as bad as it sounds, since instead of sleeping together in a double bed we now had our own single beds. And except for sleeping, which might be during the daytime if they were working a late shift, the boarders spent very little time in their rooms.

Of course, with no hot water in the house for bathing, the atmosphere in the bedrooms got a little heavy at times. But there was a public bathhouse with hot showers for twenty-five cents in the back of Red's Barber Shop, and the men availed themselves of them at least once a week. I made some money on Saturdays by cleaning the showers and keeping them supplied with soap and towels. I also swept up the floor of the barber shop as Red cut hair, and for this I was allowed to shine shoes in the shop. Red provided the two-chair shoe shine stand and the polish and shine cloths, and I collected ten cents for each shoe shine.

Mill workers liked to spruce up on the weekends, and many of them had a regular routine of getting a shave, shower and shoe shine every Saturday. Sometimes I made a dollar or more in a day, and once in a great while I even got a twenty-five cent tip. When you consider that I could go to the matinee in Gastonia and see a comedy , newsreel, serial and a cowboy movie for ten cents, then have two hamburgers and an RC Cola at the Crystal Palace for fifteen cents, that wasn't a bad tip.

In those days the average textile worker made about fifteen dollars a week, depending on his job, when he worked full time. Mama charged each of her boarders three dollars a week if they went home on weekends, or four dollars a week if they lived with us seven days a week. This included two meals a day and a sack lunch to take with them to the mill. It didn't include laundry, that was fifty cents a week extra if they wanted it. Mama couldn't do all the work herself. She did all the cooking and some of the cleaning, but she had a colored lady, Mrs. Williams, who came in every day and helped with the cleaning and did the laundry. I don't know how much Mama paid her, but I do know that she let her pack up the leftovers from the evening meal and take them home to her family. Mrs. Williams always brought a clean white cloth with her in the morning, and left with it tied up and hung from a broomstick across her shoulder when she left at night.

Most of Mama's boarders were good, hardworking family men, but every now and then she got one who liked to drink and kick up his heels on a Saturday night. Mama had strict rules against drinking, gambling or cursing in her house, so if they wanted to get drunk they had to do it somewhere else and sober up before they came home. Otherwise they were invited to go live somewhere else. North Carolina at that time had local option on the sale of alcohol and alcoholic beverages, and the voters of each county decided whether to go wet or dry. Our county, Gaston County, was completely dry, but legal beer and whiskey were for sale just ten miles away in Mecklenberg County. Men who wanted to drink, and couldn't drink at home, would often go to Charlotte after work on Friday, buy whiskey or beer and take it down to the South Fork River at Penhook to drink it. Usually they would build a fire to sit around, and sometimes they would put out a few set-hooks to catch catfish.

Johnny Matthews was not a hard drinker. In the years he lived with us I never saw him drunk. But he did like his beer, and on most Friday nights he could be found down by the river with some of the other men, sitting around the fire drinking beer while he cooked up a big pot of catfish stew.

When I was fourteen years old I talked him into taking me with him one night, telling Mama that we were going fishing. Which was true, as far as it went. Of course, he wouldn't let me drink any beer, but after helping catch and clean the fish, and peeling potatoes for the catfish stew, I did get to eat some stew out of an empty can that still smelled a little like beer. I felt very grown up, but pretty soon I went to sleep by the fire and slept until we were ready to go home. When I woke up I was convinced that I had a hangover.

Although they were good friends and roommates, our two longtime women boarders were not at all alike.

Eudora was a plain, almost homely woman, with sharp features and a long nose and chin that curved slightly toward each other, making her look a little bit like a witch in the "Wizard of Oz". But her personality was anything but witchlike. She was a warm, friendly person, who always had time to talk to us young people, and seemed genuinely interested in the things we did and hoped to do. About thirty-five years old and a high school graduate, she was an avid reader and had a sizable collection of books that she shared with me, introducing me to Tom Sawyer and Robinson Crusoe and Treasure Island among others, long before we read them in school. She was from Wilmington, North Carolina, down near the Atlantic coast. I don't know whether she had any living family, I never heard her say anything about them if she did. But in the time that she lived with us before I left home I never knew her to go back there for a visit.

Alexandria, on the other hand, was a beautiful girl. She was probably in her early to middle twenties, with black hair and eyes, a pretty face and a shapely figure. She was friendly enough, but rather reserved and quiet. Although

I'm sure she could have had her pick of any of the eligible bachelors in Lowell, she never went out on dates. Her home was in Spartanburg, South Carolina, only about seventy-five miles from Lowell, and once or twice a month she would catch the Greyhound bus from Gastonia and go home for the weekend. I imagine she had a boyfriend there, but she never talked about it.

They were two nice ladies, and Mama took special care of them as if they were her own daughters. They had the best bedroom in the house, between the living room and the kitchen, and close to the bathroom. And she made sure that there was always plenty of hot water for their baths in the reservoir on her stove.

Mama also kept one bedroom for married couples, and as a rule they made excellent boarders. Usually both husband and wife worked in the mill, and Mama preferred it that way, since the wife wasn't lying around the house all day. The only real problem she ever had was with a couple where the wife didn't work. The man was in his late forties or early fifties, and his wife was about half his age. She was cheap looking, wore too much makeup and dresses that were too tight for her. She laid around all day reading "True Love Story" magazines and painting her fingernails and toenails. When she began making eyes at some of the men boarders, Mama could see an explosion coming and asked them to leave. They didn't give her an argument about leaving, which was a pretty good indication that it had happened to them before.

Growing up in a boarding house had its advantages and disadvantages. It was crowded, to say the least, with very little living space of your own and almost no privacy. Just one drawer of your own in a chest of drawers was a luxury. But that was offset to a large extent by the advantages gained from living with a variety of people. People with different backgrounds, different beliefs and ideas. It was like being part of a big, but constantly changing, extended family. While there were occasional personality clashes and little minor tiffs, most of the time everybody got along well together, and I think I grew up a more well-rounded person from living in Mama's boarding house.

16

Once A Farmer...

For someone who had been a farmer all his life, Daddy adjusted very quickly to life in a mill village. He worked the first shift at the mill, going to work at seven in the morning and coming home at three in the afternoon. From then until suppertime he worked in his garden or did a few things around the house. In the evenings he could always be found in the living room with his rocking chair pulled up close to the little table model radio, his chewing tobacco spittoon by his side, listening to "Amos 'n Andy", "Lum and Abner", and "Fibber McGee and Molly".

His work at the mill wasn't too hard. His first job had been as porter and sweeper, which involved moving materials around the mill and keeping the floors swept clean so that the yarn and the finished cloth didn't get dirty. But about a year after starting work he was lucky enough to get a real plum of a job for a man of his age – running the Dope Wagon.

The Dope Wagon didn't sell dope, but was a lunch wagon that went through the mill three or four times on each shift, selling packaged sandwiches, candy bars, cakes, gum and soft drinks to the other workers at their work stations. It got its name from the fact that it had soft drinks like Coca Cola, or "dopes" as they were called by most southerners. When Coca Cola first came on the market there were widespread rumors that it contained small amounts of cocaine to give it its "kick", and this led to the nickname, "Coke", and later to "Dope". After a while all soft drinks came to be called dopes.

Daddy enjoyed running the Dope Wagon. The job didn't pay much, but it carried a certain amount of prestige, and allowed him to circulate all through the mill and talk to the people at their different jobs, unlike workers such as the weavers, who were virtually chained to their looms in order to keep them all running. They were glad to see him coming down the aisles, and the women kidded him and pretended to flirt with him, which was good for his ego.

There was an unwritten but clearly understood caste system among textile mill workers. At the bottom of the totem pole were the menial jobs such as the porters and sweepers. Then came the backbone of every mill – the weavers. They were responsible for keeping the looms running and actually weaving the cloth, which was the whole reason for the mill's existence.

Each weaver had from ten to twenty looms, in rows which were called "sides", and it was his or her job to keep them fed with the bobbins of "filling" for the shuttle that flew back and forth at a very high speed to intertwine with the warp and weave the cloth. They also had to stop a loom when there was a break in the filling or damage to the warp, repair the damage and start up the loom again. Since they were paid by the "pick", which was one passage of the shuttle through the warp as recorded on the pick counter, it was important to keep as many of the looms running as much of the time as possible. It was nerve-wracking work, and they earned every penny they were paid. Women often made the best weavers, as they seemed to stand up under the strain better than a lot of men.

Just above the weavers and only slightly below the loom fixers in the pecking order, were the cloth graders. Working in a spotlessly clean room on the ground level of the mill, next to the finished goods warehouse, the cloth graders, who were almost always women, took the rolls of cloth that were brought to them from the looms and ran the cloth over a light fixture that showed up any flaws or imperfections in the material. They marked any defects to be cut out of the roll, and passed any rolls that were flawless.

Their work was not physically demanding, since they did it sitting down, but it was mentally strenuous, as a mistake on their part could result in the loss of a substantial amount of money for the company.

Next to the shift foremen, or "second hands" as they were called (a corruption of "section hand") the elite of a mill were the loom fixers. Usually men who had worked as weavers for several years until they learned all about the mechanical working of the looms, it was up to them to keep these machines in good working order and to fix any breakdowns or malfunctions that occurred when they were running. Since an idle loom produced no picks, it was up to the loom fixer to get it back in service as fast as possible. Each loom fixer serviced the looms of three or four weavers and was paid an override on each weaver's picks, giving them an incentive to get the repairs done quickly. On average, a loom fixer earned about twenty percent more than a weaver.

Just as there was status involved in the different jobs in a mill, there was also status among the workers of different types of mills. The lowest were the spinning mills that spun the cotton into thread or yarn, and whose workers were called "lint-heads" because of the cotton lint that permeated their workplace and collected in their hair and on their clothing. Next were the cotton mill workers who produced cloth made of cotton.   And finally the elite (at least in their own opinion) workers in the so-called silk mills.   These mills made cloth such as rayon, crepe and taffeta out of synthetic fibers.   And sometimes they even wove some cloth out of actual silk. The Art Cloth mill was one of these silk mills.

Although Daddy liked working in the mill, each spring about planting time the genes inherited from generations of tillers of the soil made their presence known and he felt an irresistible urge to put seeds in the ground. Luckily he had some ground to put them in.

Our house was on Black Street, at the corner of Black and Linebarger, and a gully ran between it and the house on the corner of Linebarger. The gentle hillsides on both sides of the gully were on our property, giving Daddy almost half an acre of land for his garden. It was good soil, as North Carolina soil goes.   In that part of the state it's mostly hard red clay, but years of water runoff down the hillsides and into the gully had deposited silt and topsoil that had enriched this particular patch of ground and make it easier to till.

Of course Daddy didn't have a mule and a plow to turn the ground, so he got himself a hand plow, with a big wheel in front and the plow behind it, and handlebars like plow-handles for pushing it. As soon as the time was right for planting he laboriously plowed his furrows along the contour of both hillsides. When I got big enough I helped him with the plowing by tying a rope to each end of the wheel's axle, then wrapping it around my shoulder and pulling as he pushed. This speeded things up considerably.

He planted corn, tomatoes, beans, peas, cucumbers, okra and both sweet and Irish potatoes, among other things, and spent every evening after work weeding and thinning and cultivating. As each thing ripened, we picked it and gave it to Mama for the table, or for canning in half-gallon fruit jars. I didn't especially enjoy the work, but I did get a lot of satisfaction at seeing the fruits of our labors. And I can see now that Daddy's garden saved Mama a lot of money in running her boarding house.

One spring when I was about ten years old Daddy rewarded me for helping him by giving me a small piece of the garden for my own, to plant anything I liked. After a lot of thought I decided to plant peanuts. Peanuts were usually grown a little farther south, in Georgia or Alabama, and Daddy warned me that they might not do so well in our soil and climate. But I decided to try them anyway. He showed me how to plant them, and when they came up and blossomed near the ground, he told me to rake soil over the blossoms to cover them up. I couldn't believe that was right, and was sure it would kill them. But I did as he said, and when it was time to harvest them I pulled them up. And sure enough, there near the roots was a peanut where each blossom had been.

I picked them and let them dry, then roasted them in their shells in Mama's oven. I got a couple gallons of roasted nuts, and put them up in little brown bags to sell. I had visions of making a lot of money, but sales weren't very good, and my friends and I ended up eating up all the profits.

I guess I didn't inherit my Daddy's farming gene, as I've never had any real urge to farm. Or maybe I'm the exception that proves the rule to the old adage, "You can take the boy out of the country, but you can't take the country out of the boy."

17

Tent Meeting Tonight

Like the Negro slaves in the South before the Civil War, whose lot on this earth was so hopeless that they embraced the white man's religion which promised a better life in the hereafter, the poor whites during the Depression clutched at any straw that might hold out hope for a Promised Land of milk and honey after they crossed over the Great Divide. They were a fertile field for any preacher who claimed to be able to show them the way to this land, and many men with a gift of gab, and the money to make a down payment on a tent, became traveling Evangelists.

That's not to say that all traveling Evangelists were charlatans. Some of them were sincere, devout and godly men. But unfortunately there were many who were not, and were in it only for whatever money they could cajole and squeeze out of their audiences. These latter "preachers" were mostly uneducated, some barely literate, but they could read the Bible well enough to select a passage to use as the foundation for their particular doctrine, and would expound on it at length, threatening anyone who didn't believe as they did with hellfire and damnation. Then, after the trickle of nickels, dimes and pennies in the collection plate had dried up, they would fold their tent and move on the next town, to be followed within a few days by another Evangelist with a different tent and a different doctrine.

About halfway between Art Cloth and Lowell was an old baseball diamond. Before the Depression it had been used by Art Cloth's team in one of the semi-pro industrial leagues that were very popular in the South at that time. When the mill shut down, the team folded, and the traveling Evangelists found the unused ball park an excellent place to pitch their tents. And we young boys found the tent meetings good entertainment, especially since they were free.

When the evening's service was well under way, we would crawl under the back of the tent and sit down behind the last row of folding chairs. Usually by that time the crowd would have been worked up to a fever pitch and some of them would be speaking strange words that we couldn't understand, but which the preacher called, "speaking in tongues", and as their fervor increased they would roll on the dirt floor of the tent while the preacher "praised the Lord" and urged them on.

When he judged the time to be right, the preacher would call for a hymn to be sung and would ask the sinners in the crowd to come down to the front to be saved. Sometimes there would be a special healing service, with a laying-on of hands on the sick and crippled. Perhaps it was just hypnosis, or maybe trickery of some kind, but on more than one occasion I saw a man or woman go down to the preacher on crutches and walk away without them after he had gone through his laying-on of hands. Although I tended to scoff at these rituals, I have to admit that they gave me something to think about.

Not all the traveling Evangelists were men. There were a few women preachers. One of them, who called herself Sister Alma, got tired of traveling and decided to settle down in our county. Finding an old empty one-room school house in Dallas, she moved into it and established her Church of the Holy Spirit. She had made quite a few converts in the area, including my sister Belle and her husband Walter, and at first her new church showed signs of growing and prospering.

Sister Alma was a tall, handsome woman, about thirty-five years old, with fair skin and coal black hair that hung down to her shoulders, contrasting dramatically with the flowing white robes that she wore in the pulpit. Her traveling companion and business manager was a short balding middle aged man name Brother Murray. He kept in the background, handling the money and taking care of the day to day business of the church, leaving the preaching and public relations to Sister Alma. Apparently, however, he performed at least one more service for her.

When it reached the point where even Sister Alma's flowing robes couldn't conceal the fact that she was several months pregnant, her flock began to desert her. Even the most loyal among them were not willing to accept the idea of another Immaculate Conception. Belle was one of the last to give up on her, and was very disillusioned by the turn of events. She couldn't understand why they didn't just get married, but then she reasoned that probably one or both of them were already married to somebody else.

Before the baby was born, Sister Alma and Brother Murray packed up and moved to another part of the state. The traveling Evangelists continued to come through town and pitch their tents on the ball field, but I lost interest in them as I got busy with other things.

18

Pulling My Own Weight

Even though times were slowly getting better by nineteen-thirty-five, the year that I was eleven years old, and Daddy was working full time and Mama was taking in boarders, money was still very tight. Mama had had to put a hot water heater in the bathroom, and replace the old icebox with an electric refrigerator in order to modernize her boarding house, and she and Daddy had bought a second-hand car, a 1932 Buick roadster with a rumble seat, so that he could take her grocery shopping at Piggly Wiggly's in Gastonia.

There was no extra money for foolishness like candy and cokes or movies, so if I wanted these things I had to work to earn the money for them. I found several ways to do it. The first was by helping out on a newspaper route.

There were two newspapers in our area in those days, *The Gastonia Gazette*, which was a weekly paper then, and *The Charlotte Observer* which was delivered daily and on Sunday. The *Observer* cost twenty cents a week delivered, twelve cents of which went to the newspaper company and eight cents to the delivery boy. Even during the worst of the depression the local Art Cloth route had forty or so customers, and by the time I started helping out on the route in the summer of nineteen-thirty-five that number had grown to sixty.

A fifteen year old boy named James Thomas had the route. He paid me a dollar a week to help him, and to deliver the papers by myself when he was away from home, or had something else to do, which seemed to be a good part of the time. Delivering the papers during the week wasn't bad, as the paper was usually thin enough so that I could get all of them in my sack at one time. But Sunday was a different story. With all the various sections, including comics and Sunday supplements, each paper was often two or three inches thick and I could only carry about ten of them at a time. Even with two of us working it was quite a job, but when I had to do it by myself it took about two hours and I was worn out by the time I was through.

Although I was glad to get the dollar a week, and didn't mind the work, the main reason I helped James was because he promised to give the route to me when he gave it up in a year or so. With sixty customers I could earn almost five dollars a week if I collected from everybody. That was more than my Daddy had made some weeks during the worst of the depression.

James turned sixteen in nineteen-thirty-six and gave up the route to take a job working in a grocery store. That would have worked out fine for me, since I was twelve years old that summer and old enough to have the route. Except that he didn't give it to me. When I asked him about it he said another kid had offered him twenty-five dollars for it and that he was going to sell it to him. I was stunned and sick with disappointment. I had worked so hard for that route, and now he was going to sell it to someone else.

At first I thought of offering him more for it, maybe thirty dollars. But I didn't have thirty dollars and didn't know where I could get it. And then I got mad. He had promised the route to me and I had done everything he asked me to do, over and above what he paid me the dollar

93

a week for, just so I could get it. It wasn't fair, and the more I thought about it the madder I got. It just didn't seem like any way to run a newspaper to me, and I decided to see the Circulation Manager and tell him what I thought of it.

The next morning I put on my best shirt and overalls and took the P&N train to Charlotte. I had looked up the address of the *Charlotte Observer's* offices on the editorial page of the paper, and luckily it was within walking distance of the P&N station. I got there about ten o'clock in the morning and told the woman at the front desk that I wanted to see the Circulation Manager about a paper route. Somewhat to my surprise she sent me right into his office.

His name was Mr. Morton, and he turned out to be a very nice man. He listened patiently as I told him my story, and when I finished he asked me if I really wanted the paper route, and if I was sure I could handle it. I assured him the answer was yes to both questions. Then he told me that a delivery boy on a route had no right to sell the route to someone else, or even to give it to them for that matter. That was up to the Circulation Manager, although he did take into consideration the delivery boy's recommendation as to his successor. But it was strictly against company policy for anyone to sell or offer to sell a route. Then he had me fill out an Application Form and put down the name of two references. I put down the names of my school principal, Mr. Helton, and my Sunday School teacher, Miss Grace Jones. When I handed it back to him he told me that I would hear from him in a few days.

When I got home that day I didn't tell anyone but Mama what I had done. James was off on one of his trips, so I didn't have to face him right away. By the time he got back the route was no longer his. Two days after I went to see him Mr. Morton drove up to our house and talked to Mama and me. When he left I had the paper route. I thought James would be mad and maybe try to beat me up or something, but I guess Mr. Morton must have talked to him and scared him a little for trying to sell the route, for he never said a word to me about it. He still had some money coming from customers who were behind in their payments, so when I collected it I put it in an envelope and left it at his house for him.

Theoretically, I should have made almost five dollars a week on the route when I took it over, but it didn't always work out that way. When I collected for the papers on Saturday of each week, the newspaper company got their money first, twelve cents for each paper I delivered. I got what was left. Almost all my customers were honest, hard working people who wouldn't try to beat me out of my money. But times were still not back to normal, and people sometimes lost their jobs or moved to another mill town, and moved away without paying me. I hated to cut anybody off, and often let some of them go four or five weeks without paying before I stopped their paper. Since I still had to pay the company for those papers, my weekly income averaged more like four dollars than five.

Out of this paper route money I kept fifty cents a week for spending money, put aside money to buy my clothes, and gave the rest to Mama to help with the household budget. Later, when the route had grown and I was finding other ways to add to its proceeds, I started a savings account in a bank in Gastonia to save money for college.

I delivered the *Observer* seven days a week for the next four years and had some interesting experiences.

There were a lot of dogs on the route and most of them were harmless, all bark and no bite. But one of my customers, a foreign looking man who lived in a house by himself, had an Eskimo Spitz that used to lay in ambush for me. He never barked or growled, but would lie under the front porch until I got close to the house, but not quite close enough to throw the paper, then he would come charging out and try to bite my leg.

After being bitten a couple of times I solved that problem. I cut off a broom handle to a length of about three feet and stashed it under the porch of the house next door to the Spitz. The next morning I picked it up and carried it with me as I approached the house where he lay in wait. When he charged out at me I whacked him on the nose with the stick, just hard enough to stop him in his tracks but not really hurt him. After that I always carried the stick when I approached his house, and left it next door as I went back up the street, ready for the next day. I didn't have any trouble with him after that.

But my most frightening experience was the morning I surprised the Negro man in the drug store.

Our village "shopping center" consisted of three stores located at one end of the village, just where the road to Lowell crossed the P&N Railroad tracks. They were Gilliams' Grocery, which also housed the branch Post Office; Red's Barber Shop and Bathhouse; and the combination Drug Store and Poolhall (when Gaston County legalized the sale of beer in nineteen-thirty-four it also became the closest thing that we had to a tavern). The street in front of these stores had about fifty feet of the only paved sidewalk in Art Cloth, and every day the *Observer's* delivery truck left my bundle of papers on the sidewalk in front of the drug store. Every morning about five o'clock I would walk up to the store, cut the string on the bundle and load my delivery bag.

It was dark at that hour of the morning, and one morning I walked up to the drug store, still half asleep, and bent over to cut the string with my pocket knife. As I did I looked at the drug store window and saw that the glass had been broken and that there was a big hole in it. Then I saw the Negro man behind the counter, with his hand in the open cash register drawer. He looked up and saw me at almost the same instant, and I don't know who scared who the most. I let out a yell and started running away from the store, and as I did I heard glass breaking as he jumped through the broken window and took off in the direction of the railroad tracks.

The Deputy Sheriff, Mr. Maddux, lived in the first house down Main Street from the stores, and I ran to it and started pounding on the door and yelling. When he woke up and came to the door I told him what I had seen and he had me wait in his living room while he got dressed. He went back to the drug store with me, but of course the man was gone by then. He said he would handle it from there and told me to go on and deliver my papers. I did, and it made a very exciting story to tell the kids at school that day.   It never happened again, but from then on I approached the drug store very cautiously every morning, whistling and making a lot of noise as I came up the street.

I also owe my love of classical music to the paper route.

I collected for the papers on Saturday morning, in order to have the *Observer's* money when Mr. Morton came around Saturday afternoon. It was hard work, as I often had to go back to the same customer's house two or three times before I caught them at home. Usually by the time I had collected all I could and settled up with Mr. Morton, I was pretty tired and would go home and flop down in front of the radio to rest.

In those days one of the big companies (I can't remember which one) sponsored the broadcast of a Young Peoples' Symphony Concert from Carnegie Hall in New York on Saturday afternoons. Although I didn't really understand it at first, I found the music soothing and relaxing and I looked forward to it every week. As I got older I bought some used classical records and played them on the old wind-up Victrola that one of the boarders had left with us. I never studied music, but I acquired a taste for the classics from these Saturday afternoon concerts. And even now, when things get a little hectic, I find the best way to forget my problems for a few minutes or a few hours, is with Grieg or Beethoven or Mozart.

When I turned sixteen and was old enough to work in the mill after school, I had over a hundred customers on the paper route and was making about eight dollars a week. When I asked him, Mr. Morton agreed to let my younger brother, Wallace, have the route. Wallace worked it until he went into the Navy in nineteen-forty-four.

19

A Cowboy At Last

Ironically, after my earlier experience of running away from home to go to Texas, one of my ways of earning money when I was twelve years old was by herding cows.

During the depression people did anything they could to survive. Everybody planted a garden and raised corn and potatoes and vegetables, and a lot of them had milk cows. Between the village of Art Cloth and the South Fork River there were several hundred acres of vacant land. Many years ago there had had been a small village called Penhook along the river bank, with a grist mill for grinding corn. But influenza or some other epidemic disease had wiped out most of the population and what was left moved on. There were still parts of a few stone chimneys standing, and overgrown piles of rubble where homes had been, and an old graveyard with broken tombstones and stone markers showing dates of death going back to the eighteen hundreds. It was a favorite place for us to play Cowboys and Indians when I was younger, and it turned out to be perfect for herding cattle.

We still had Mama's old cow, Bessy, and Grandpa Ash had given us a young heifer that had just had her first calf, so we had two milk cows. Daddy built a rough sort of stable for them out on the edge of the village, and a rail fence to make a corral. When school was out for the summer I took the cows out of the corral and let them graze on the thick grass down toward the river. It wasn't long until other people in the village started using the corral for their cows, and pretty soon some of them asked me if I would graze their cows for them. That's how I got into the cow herding business. I charged twenty-five cents per week per cow, and at one point I had sixteen cows in my herd.

Cows are sort of like people in one way, they follow the leader. It didn't take me long to find out that one of the cows was the boss, and that the others followed her. So we put a bell around this cow's neck and I drove them down toward the river every morning. I didn't have to stay with them all the time, since they couldn't get into any real trouble and wouldn't stray too far from home. But in grazing they would work their way some distance from where I left them, so I went to find them two or three times a day, guided by the bell, to make sure they were all there and all okay. About an hour before milking time in the evening I would round them all up and drive them back to the corral.

I continued to herd cows even after school started, while I was still in Grade School and could use my lunch hour to go and check on them. It meant that I had to get up very early in the morning to deliver my papers and drive the cows to pasture before going to school. But I didn't mind. And since I had to go down through Penhook every morning and evening anyway, I discovered another way to make a little extra money and put some more food on the table. Catching rabbits.

There were a lot of wild rabbits around the old ruins and in the grassy fields of Penhook, so I built several rabbit traps ("rabbit boxes" as we called them) and set them out in likely spots along the route of my cattle drives. I would bait the traps with pieces of apple or carrot when I rounded up the cows in the evening, and collect any rabbits that I had caught when I drove them out in the morning. Since it was pretty hard to carry a squirming live rabbit, I got quite good at pulling one out of a trap by its hind legs and breaking its neck with a quick blow to the back of the neck with the side of my hand.

Rabbits were considered next to chicken as a delicacy by most Southerners, so I didn't have too much trouble selling them for twenty-five cents apiece. Of course I kept enough for our own table. Mama could cook them so that they tasted almost like chicken. In fact, since my Daddy claimed he didn't like rabbit, she sometimes would cook only two of the rabbit's legs, along with the rest of it, and tell him it was chicken, and he never seemed to know the difference.

I gave up herding cows when I went into High School, although I still caught a few rabbits, and one of the other boys in the village took it over. By that time the worst of the Depression was over and a lot of the villagers had sold their cows, so the business wasn't as lucrative as it had been. But it was good while it lasted, and my college savings account had grown quite a bit.

20

"On My Honor, I Will Do My Best.........."

When I was twelve years old I joined the Boys' Scouts. The Woodlawn (Art Cloth) First Baptist Church sponsored a local Boys' Scout Troop, and we met every Tuesday evening in the auditorium of the school house. Our Grade School Principal, Mr. Helton, was the Scoutmaster.

I enjoyed Scouting very much. Other than school and Church, it was the only organization I had ever belonged to, and I liked the feeling of being a part of something, of being able to say that this was "my" Scout Troop. At our weekly meetings we studied the Scouting Manual, learned the Oath and Motto and Laws, and worked on Merit Badges so that we could progress through the ranks from Tenderfoot to the coveted Eagle Scout. When the studying was done we played rough-house games such as "King of the Hill" and "Capture the Flag", which often got a little out of hand and resulted in a few bruises and an occasional bloody nose. But that was all a part of the fun of it, and the process of becoming Scouts. Once a month we went to a Court of Honor at one of the Troops in our Piedmont Council, on a rotating basis, for the presentation of Merit Badges and other awards that had been earned since the last meeting.

A few of the older boys in our Troop had complete Scout uniforms, but because of the cost most of us started out with just a cap, a neckerchief with a leather slide, and a sash for our Merit Badges. However, by saving part of my spending money from my paper route, I managed to get the rest of my uniform by my second year in the Troop. It was a summer uniform, with short pants and short-sleeved shirt, but with our North Carolina weather I could wear it most of the year.

Scouting also made possible the only real vacation that I had while I was growing up. That was in the summer of nineteen-thirty-seven, when I was thirteen years old.

The Piedmont Council of the Boys' Scouts of America operated a summer Scout Camp on Lake Lanier, near Tryon, North Carolina, in the foothills of the Blue Ridge Mountains. Every year the Scouts in each troop in the Council were given the opportunity of spending a week at the camp. The cost for the week was seven dollars per Scout, which was more than most of us could afford, but the Baptist Church that sponsored us contributed half the cost, as well as transportation, so it only cost me three dollars and fifty cents, which I was able to raise from my paper route and other jobs. Of course, I had to pay my brother Wallace to deliver my papers and take care of the cows. But Mama let me skip my contribution to the family pot that week, so I was able to handle it without borrowing against my future earnings.

The week at the Boy Scout Camp ran from Saturday noon until the next Saturday morning, and on the day that we were to leave I was at the schoolhouse bright and early with my uniform on and my knapsack packed. One of the members of the Church had an old "A" Model Ford truck with a stake bed, and the six of us from our Troop that were going to Camp piled into the back of it. A couple of the boys had been to the Camp before, and they were acting very nonchalant, putting their heads on their knapsacks and pretending to sleep. But the rest of us were so excited that we were practically jumping up and down.

Our route to the Camp took us west through Gastonia, Kings Mountain, Shelby and Forest City. Then just before the road turned northwest toward Hendersonville, we turned south, and in just a few minutes we arrived at Camp Lanier, the whole trip having taken less than two hours.

We rounded a bend in the road and there it was before us – a beautiful clear lake surrounded by tall pines and firs, and on its banks were neat rows of tent cottages and log buildings laid out around what appeared to be a parade ground. The American flag flew from a tall flagpole in front of one of the biggest of the log buildings, with the flag of the Piedmont Council of the Boy Scouts beneath it.

The first thing that struck me about the camp was how neat and orderly it looked. The tent-cottages were shaded by tall pine trees, and their canvas sides were rolled up, all at exactly the same height, to allow the cool breezes to pass through them. Even at this distance I could see the cots on the wooden floors of the cottages, all neatly made up and lined up in two rows of four. The area around and between the cottages was covered with a layer of pine needles, and there was no sign of any paper or other trash to spoil the natural beauty.

Along the lake in front of the camp, an area about a hundred yards long and twenty-five yards wide was enclosed by heavy rope and floating buoys to form the swimming pool. Just beyond one end of the swimming area there were several canoes lined up along the bank. I had never paddled a canoe before, and could hardly wait to try it.

Our driver stopped the truck in front of the building with the flags, and went inside. He came out a few minutes later with a young man in a Scout uniform, who introduced

Camp Lanier

himself as Jim Timberlake, our Counselor for the week that we would be there. He directed our driver to one of the tent-cottages and told us to unload our gear. Leading us inside the cottage he checked off our names on his clipboard, and assigned each of us a cot. Then he spent the next half hour explaining our schedule of activities.

During our stay we would have swimming, physical training, hiking, nature study and canoeing every day. In between these activities we would work on the Merit Badges that we needed for our next rank. And, of course, there would be breakfast, dinner and supper in the messhall at seven a.m., twelve noon, and six p.m. In the evenings after supper there would be a campfire that we would sit around as the Counselors told stories. Lights-out was at ten o'clock.

The Counselor pointed to the bulletin board on the wall just to the left of the front entrance to the cottage, and indicated the schedule of our activities on it, along with a map of the camp. Since there were no organized activities, except meals, until Church Services on Sunday morning, we were free to explore the camp or do anything else we liked, just as long as we didn't go off into the woods without one of the Counselors as a guide. Jim said he would be sleeping in our cottage with us, and pointed out his living and sleeping area in one of the front corners of the cottage. Then he dismissed us.

Most of us new campers had the same idea. First we had to find the latrines, and then the messhall. There were four latrines in the camp, and one of them was located quite close to our cottage. Although it smelled of disinfectant, it was clean and comfortable, with toilet seats on the holes in the latrine, and shower stalls with cold water showers. We were told later that this camp had been built by workers from the Civilian Conservation Corps.

It was easy to find the messhall, as it was one of the biggest buildings in the camp, and there were appetizing odors coming from it as the cooks prepared the midday meal. The doors were kept locked until mealtime, but looking through the front door screen we could see rows of tables covered with white oilcloth. There were no eating utensils on the tables, but each one held two glass pitchers for water or milk.

We still had about an hour to kill before dinner, so a couple of the other boys and I went exploring around the camp. We found another large building that had a sign over its front door that said, "Activities". We went inside and found that it had a number of tables of various sizes, chairs, and work benches. We quickly figured out that this was where we would work on crafts and other projects for Merit Badges. It was very interesting, but I was anxious to see the canoes, so we went down by the waterfront.

There were eight canoes, all about the same size, and two larger ones. A Counselor who happened by told us that the smaller ones were two-man canoes, although they could be handled by one man if he was really proficient at it. The big ones were war canoes, and would carry up to six paddlers sitting in a row from front to back, with three paddling on each side. Unlike the canoes in stories I had read about Indians, these weren't made of birch bark. They were made of canvas stretched tightly over a frame of small limber tree limbs, and coated with several coats of clear varnish to stiffen the canvas and make it waterproof. Each canoe was decorated with colorful Indian designs, and I could hardly wait to try them out.

Tearing ourselves away from the canoes, we walked on around the Camp and found a clearing at the edge of the woods where the nightly campfires were built. Pieces of charred wood from the last campfire were scattered on the ashes of a hundred old fires at the center of the clearing, and logs about a foot thick radiated out from the ashes in concentric circles, like ripples from a stone thrown in still water, forming a rough sort of amphitheater and providing seats for the Scouts and Counselors.

Then we heard our first bugle call since arriving at the camp. None of us had a watch, but since it had to be about twelve o'clock, it was pretty easy to figure out that it was chow call. It even sounded like a chow call, with the bugle seeming to say, "Soupy, soupy, soupy!". We made a mad dash for the messhall and arrived there just as one of the counselors was unlocking the door. He told us to slow down and take it easy, then showed us the table that would be ours for the rest of our stay. After all the other Scouts arrived and were seated, the Camp Chaplain said Grace and then each table in turn went through the chow line.

As we went down the line in front of the hot tables the cook and the kitchen helpers, who were Scouts that spent the whole summer at the camp in exchange for working, ladled the food into the compartments in our mess tins. It was good, and the portions were generous. There were weenies and pork and beans, creamed corn and turnip greens, corn bread, and canned peaches for dessert. When we got back to our table the KP's had filled the pitchers with cold milk.   By this time we had worked up a good appetite and we polished off our food in short order. When we finished we took our empty trays back to the end of the chow line and rinsed them in a big tub of hot water.

After dinner we visited the little store in the Administration Building. I bought some postcards with pretty pictures of the camp and the lake and the surrounding area to send back to the folks at home. They cost a penny each and stamps for them were also a penny. When we got back to our cottage I sat on my bunk and wrote and addressed one to Mama and another to Grandma and Grandpa Ash. Then I got out my Boy Scout Manual and tried to study for some of the Merit Badges that I was working on. But the long ride and the fresh air had made me sleepy, so I put the book down and took a nap.

I must have slept for about two hours. When I woke up a couple of the other guys and I went exploring again down around the lake beyond the canoes, where we couldn't get lost. We saw a mama raccoon with her two little pups, and several other small animals, including an otter that was playing in the water just off the shore of the lake. We picked up smooth stones along the beach, and one of the fellows found a piece of flint, shaped exactly like an Indian arrowhead, which had probably been planted there by one of the Counselors just to whet our interest in learning more about the Cherokees that had lived there not too long ago.

Coming as we did from a small mill village with undeveloped land around it, we weren't city boys and had seen lots of small wild animals. But we had never seen them in such a beautiful and unspoiled setting. Somehow this made them more interesting. The water of the lake was clear and blue, and the air fresh and clean. And everything was so quiet. We had become so accustomed to the noise of the mills, when they were working, that at first it seemed like something was missing. The only sounds on the unpolluted air was the rustle of the wind in the pines, the cries of wild birds calling across the water to their mates, and the occasional bark of an animal that might have been a wolf but was probably a coyote.

Caught up in the beauty of the place, and finding something more of interest all the time, we ending up hiking almost halfway around the lake and just barely made it back to camp in time for supper. Since Saturday was a day off for most of the Counselors, there was no campfire that night. Which was perhaps just as well, since

110

we were all dead tired. I went to bed as soon as it was dark and slept until reveille the next morning. Except for morning Church Services in the little Chapel, Sunday was pretty much the same as the day before. But on Monday morning our week's activities began in earnest.

Beginning with the bugler blowing reveille at six o'clock in the morning, and Jim Timberlake rousting us out for thirty minutes of PT on the parade ground with all the Scouts from the other troops, until Taps that evening, we were kept busy just about every minute of the day. We went hiking, swimming, canoeing, and worked on Merit Badges in the Activities Building. I was working on a Merit Badge on Indian Lore, and worked on making a pair of moccasins from a kit that I had bought at the camp store.

After dark the Counselors lit the campfire and we all sat on the logs around it and sang Scouting songs, and listened as they told stories. When the fire died down, one of them produced some marshmallows and we toasted them over the coals on long green twigs until they were black and melting. I enjoyed everything about that week at Camp, but next to Canoeing I think I liked the Campfires best.

The rest of the week went by much too fast. I improved my swimming enough to pass my Lifesaving Merit Badge, finished the moccasins I had started, and learned to paddle a canoe, including how to turn it right-side up and get back in it after I tipped it over. By the time we left the next Saturday morning, I was well tanned and my body and my mind fine-tuned and fit.

I stayed in the Boys Scouts until I was sixteen years old and reached the rank of Life Scout, just one step short of Eagle Scout rank. I had to quit then to go to work in the mill to save money for college, and never got to go back to Camp Lanier. But that week in the summer of nineteen-thirty-seven was one of the best weeks of my life.

21

A Love Affair With Flying

My love affair with flying began before I was six years old.

After the end of World War I, a lot of discharged pilots took up barnstorming. They did it partly to eke out a living, but mostly just for the love of flying. They picked up old fighter planes for practically nothing and converted them to carry passengers. Or bought second-hand Jennys with their separation bonuses and joined the fraternity of flying hoboes that crisscrossed the country before and during the depression, putting on aerial shows and taking up passengers when they could find them, for whatever the traffic would bear.

Even before we left the farm it was not unusual to see an old biplane circling overhead, sometimes so low that you could see right into the pilot's cockpit, trying to drum up interest in rides at the nearby Greenville airstrip. I was fascinated by these pilots and their airplanes, and dreamed of flying one of them myself. When I was old enough to read I read everything I could get my hands on about Fighter Aircraft and their battles in the Great War, and when I began to earn a little spending money I bought model airplane kits and built "flying" models of balsa wood and paper.

These models were powered by a strong rubber band that you wound up by turning the propeller counter-clockwise until the rubber band was twisted into a series of knots. When you released the propeller and launched the plane into the air, it sometimes would actually fly a short distance before crashing and breaking apart. But more often the rubber band broke or collapsed the fuselage of the plane before it left my hand. But undaunted, I would repair it and try again, or invest in another kit as soon as I had another dime.

But I really fell in love with flying when I was thirteen and got my first real airplane ride.

About halfway between Lowell and Charlotte was a big grassy field that was used as a landing field for private planes (it later was named Douglas Field and became Charlotte's Municipal Airport). Barnstorming pilots would often fly over our village and the others around us, sometimes dropping leaflets to try to entice people to the airfield so that they could sell rides in their planes. Sometimes two or three of them would put on an airshow, flying in close formation or performing mock dogfights, and even doing wing-walking. To me this was the most thrilling and exciting thing in the world, and I would beg Daddy to take me to the airfield to see it close up. One Sunday afternoon I finally succeeded.

By the summer of nineteen-thirty-seven the worst of the Great Depression had run its course. Hitler had come into power in Germany and war clouds were gathering over Europe, so the United States began to increase the size of its military forces. This meant more uniforms and more material to make them, so the mills began to run again.

Daddy was working five days a week, Mama was taking in more boarders and our family was financially much better off. Ella Mae and Woody and their three boys had moved to Shelby, about twenty-five miles from Lowell, where Woody was working full time at the Cleveland Cloth Mill. About once a month we went to their house for

113

SIDNEY BOLICK

Sunday dinner, with Wallace and me riding in the rumble seat of the Buick.

But Shelby wasn't where I wanted to go on this Sunday afternoon. I wanted to go to Charlotte to see the airplanes, and Daddy surprised me by agreeing to take me when I asked him to. Maybe he just wanted to drive his car, which was still new enough to him to be a novelty, but whatever the reason, I piled in with him and we drove to the airfield.

There was no show that afternoon, just one old biplane sitting on the ground with a few people standing around. The plane was painted bright red, which only partially camouflaged the patches in the canvas covering of the wings and fuselage, and had "TEX BARNES – THE FLYING COWBOY" in big white letters down both sides of the fuselage and across the bottom of the lower wing.

A tall blond man, that I correctly assumed to be the Pilot, was giving the small crowd his best sales pitch, trying to get them to shell out fifty cents for a ten minute ride over the field. He had on faded khaki coveralls, cowboy boots, a well worn leather flying jacket with buckskin tassels sewn across the front and down the outside of each sleeve, and a ten-gallon Stetson cowboy hat, making him look something like a cross between Hopalong Cassidy and Captain Eddie Rickenbacker.

He wasn't having much luck getting customers, so as Daddy and I walked up he decided to change his tactics and try to shame them into taking a ride. Looking right at me he said, "Just to show you how safe this airplane is, I'm going to take that young man there up for a free ride, and then let him tell you how he likes it. How about it, son?"

For once in my life I was almost speechless! But I recovered quickly and yelled back that I sure would like to go for a ride, if my Daddy would let me. That took a little doing, but Daddy finally said all right, after the crowd began to urge him to let me go.

I could hardly believe my good fortune. I had wanted to see the airplanes, maybe even get up close and touch one, but never in my wildest dreams had I imagined that I would get to go up for a ride in one of them!

The Pilot came forward to meet me and took me over to the airplane and showed me how to climb up on the lower wing and get in the front cockpit and buckle myself in. Barnstormers used the front cockpit for passengers because the fuselage was wider toward the front and the cockpit bigger. In fact, it was big enough for two people, so I had lots of room. For obvious reasons the flight controls had been taken out of the passenger cockpit, but there was an instrument panel with an altimeter and airspeed indicator. The curve of the cockpit above the instrument panel was padded, and just above the padding there was a big curved windscreen to protect the passengers from the blast of air from the propeller.

Turning my head around as far as I could, I watched Tex as he stepped up on the wing by the rear cockpit. Taking off his cowboy hat he put it behind his seat and replaced it with a leather flying helmet and a pair of goggles. Then, after climbing in and fastening his seat harness, he leaned his head to one side and looked at his mechanic-assistant who was standing with one hand on the propeller.

Flipping a switch in front of him the Pilot said, "Switch off, and the mechanic repeated, "Switch off" and began to turn the propeller slowly. When he had turned it one complete revolution he stopped and said, "Switch on." Tex flipped the switch back on and said, "Switch on. Contact." The mechanic repeated "Contact" and gave the propeller a hard spin, putting the whole weight of his body behind it. When the engine didn't start, they went through the whole procedure again, until on the third try the big radial engine coughed once, backfired, and then started with a roar as its seven cylinders began to fire in rotation.

I had never heard an airplane engine this close before, and the noise was almost deafening. I put my fingers in my ears for a second or two, but then took them out as the Pilot jockeyed the throttle back and forth to clear the cylinders, then pushed it up to about half power to check the magnetos. When he was satisfied that everything was all right, he throttled back and signaled to the mechanic to remove the wooden chocks that kept the plane's wheels from moving while they were starting the engine.

With the chocks removed Tex pointed the airplane straight ahead and slowly opened the throttle. The prevailing winds here at Charlotte were from the southwest so most of the takeoffs and landings were made in that direction. There were no runways on the field, but the grass had been packed down and worn away from so much traffic in the one direction that unless there was a change in the wind the pilots just followed those tracks. That's what Tex did, and as soon as we were well away from the crowd he pushed the throttle all the way forward and we began to pick up speed.

I noticed the change in the attitude of the plane as the tail came up off the ground. The trees along one side of the field, and the cars on the highway on the other side, seemed to be flashing by at a dizzying pace, and before I knew what was happening the grass of the field began to fall away below us and we were flying!

It was much different than what I had expected. In the movies airplanes seemed to take off with a roar and climb straight up with their noses pointed at the sky. But this wasn't like that at all. The nose of our plane seemed to be fixed on a point just slightly above the skyline of downtown Charlotte, and there was very little change in its attitude as we continued to climb out away from the field. But I could tell we were gaining altitude, even though I couldn't understand the markings on the altimeter in front of me, for the buildings and people and cars below us were getting smaller and smaller. We didn't seem to be going very fast either and the higher we got the slower we seemed to go, although the needle on the air speed indicator was holding steady at sixty miles an hour. I hadn't yet learned that an airplane's apparent speed over the ground is dependent upon its height above fixed objects on the ground.

Any nervousness I might have felt on the takeoff was quickly dispelled by my fascination with the feeling of flying - of seeming to be completely detached from the earth and everything on it, and of being suspended between earth and sky as we seemed to float from one point to another. I had quickly gotten used to the roar of the engine, and now as the Pilot throttled back to level out at five hundred feet its drone was steady and reassuring. When he pushed the nose down to stop his climb and level out, there was a momentary sensation of partial weightlessness, something like I had felt on some of the rides at the Gaston County Fair. But it wasn't uncomfortable, and by the time he dropped his left wing and started to turn around the airfield preparatory to landing, I found my body moving with the motion of the airplane and I began to really enjoy it.

It seemed that my first airplane ride was over much too quickly. Turning toward the airfield and pointing the nose in the direction that we had taken off, Tex pulled back on the throttle until the propeller seemed to be barely ticking over, then lowered the nose until he was holding his airspeed steady at sixty miles an hour. Although there was very little feeling of descending, objects on the ground were getting bigger very quickly, and as we neared the edge of the field the sensation of speed increased until we seemed to be moving very fast. As we flew over the crowd at about a hundred feet Tex gave the engine a short burst

117

of throttle, then pulled the throttle all the way back and raised the nose of the plane. For a moment we seemed to be standing still in that position, but then the wheels settled onto the grass in a perfect three point position with just a slight bounce.

As we rolled almost to a stop, the Pilot pushed the throttle forward and rode hard on his left rudder pedal, letting the action of the propeller's blast on the rudder swing him around until he was pointed back toward the crowd. Fishtailing first left and then right so that he could see past the plane's big nose, he taxied back to the spot where we had taken off and shut off the engine.

Not wanting to break the spell, and re-living every moment of my first flight, I sat there in the cockpit looking around me; at the wings with their canvas covering stretched taut over curved ribs, and the "N" braces and crossed wires that connected the top wing to the bottom one; at the big exhaust pipes that curved back along each side of the fuselage from the engine, leaving a black smear from a mixture of exhaust gasses and burning oil on the red canvas and partly obscuring the "T" in the word, "TEX"; and at the fluted cylinder heads that circled the engine like spokes on a wheel.

I was snapped out of it by Tex unbuckling my seat harness and saying that the ride was over, and telling me to be sure and let the crowd know how much I liked it.

He didn't have to worry about that. I was still bubbling over with excitement as I went back to where Daddy was waiting for me, and I guess I was talking a mile a minute, as he had to tell me to slow down. Tex's plan to stir up some business must have worked, for as we walked back toward our car I saw a couple men handing him some money. We didn't stay around to see him take off again, although I would have liked to. But Daddy wanted to get home in time for his regular evening radio programs, and I

First Flight!

could hardly wait to tell everybody about my airplane ride, especially Red Padgett.

Red was Clarence Padgett, Jr., and he lived just down the street from us. He was my best friend, and loved flying almost as much as I did. We built model airplanes together and talked about getting into the Air Corps. Except that he wanted to get into the Naval Air Corps flying cadet program and go to Pensacola, Florida for his training, while I had my heart set on the Army Air Corps and Randolph Field, Texas. He'd be very jealous that I had been up in an airplane before he had, and I wouldn't hesitate to remind him of it when he got a little too cocky.

If there was a turning point in my young life, that airplane ride was it. From that day on I had my heart set on learning how to fly. The best way to do that was to join the Army Air Corps, but to be accepted for Flying Cadet training you had to have at least two years of college. Since there was no way that my parents could afford to pay to send me to college, I would have to save enough money to pay for it myself. And that's what I set out to do.

22

High School – The First Year

I turned thirteen years old in the summer of nineteen-thirty-seven and entered High School in September of that year. Since we only had eleven grades, Grade School was from first grade through grade seven, and High School from the eighth through the eleventh. With my birthday coming in June I was always one of the youngest kids in my class, although usually a little bigger than most of the others. At thirteen I had not yet begun to experience the rapid growth that occurs sometimes during the teens, but I was already five-feet-six. And while I was on the skinny side at a hundred and thirty pounds, my weight was mostly muscle and I was physically quite strong.

By cutting through the woods and across the P&N Railroad tracks, Lowell High School was a little less than a mile from where we lived. So I walked to and from school. We only had a half hour for lunch, and there was no school cafeteria. Since I didn't have time to walk home and back, I either brought a lunch or bought something in the little grocery store on the main street, across the Southern Railroad tracks from the school, if I had the money. An RC Cola was a nickel, and I could get a Lance's Peanut Butter and Crackers, or a Moon Pie for another nickel, and three or four of us would sit on a bench in front of the store to eat our lunch. Not going home for lunch was the first real difference between Grade School and High School, and was the beginning of my being cut loose from my Mama's apron strings.

The other principal difference was the way we moved from one classroom to another for our different classes. In Grade School we had all our classes in the same room, but in High School we had a Home Room with a Home Room Teacher. After she took attendance in the morning we waited for the bell to ring and then jostled our way down the hall to our first period class. We only had five minutes to get from one class to another and get settled in, but those five minutes became a sort of social period, and the hallway a meeting place in which to flirt with the girls and show off for them by making smart remarks at the expense of other (and usually smaller) boys.

As freshmen we also teased the girls and pulled their braids as a way of showing our interest in them, and they would giggle and pretend to get mad and chase us down the hall. That would change as we got older, and by the time we were juniors and seniors we took advantage of each brief break between classes to find a spot out of the flow of traffic to stand quietly and hold hands with the girl that we were madly in love with at the moment.

The High School building was a two-story structure that sat on the side of a small hill, with a half basement beneath it. All of the classrooms and the Principal's office were on the ground floor, and the basement held the Chemistry, Physics and Biology Labs, and the Typing Classroom. About three-quarters of the top floor was taken up by the gymnasium and boys and girls locker rooms, and the rest by the Home Economics Department.

When I entered Lowell High School in nineteen-thirty-seven it had a total enrollment of about a hundred and fifty students, with two Freshmen Home Rooms and one each for the Sophomore, Junior and Senior Classes. Since the law only required children to go to school until they were sixteen years old, and students could be kept back as many times as necessary for them to pass the requirements for a particular grade, there was a drop in enrollment from the Freshman Class to the Sophomore, and from the Sophomore to the Junior. And a decided drop from the Junior Class to the Senior Class, as most students passed their sixteenth birthday. When I graduated in nineteen-forty-one there were only twenty-one in my graduating class.

Lowell High School drew its students from the Grade Schools at the mill villages of Smyre and McAdenville, as well as Lowell and Art Cloth. All the way through Grade School I had been in classes with the same classmates, but my first year in High School I found myself among many kids that I didn't know. It didn't take long to get acquainted with them, and some of them came to be really good friends.

At thirteen, most of us had gone through puberty, and were taking a good look at members of the opposite sex. It was interesting to observe that some of the girls I had known most of my life, and who seemed almost sexless to me, were very popular with boys from the other mill villages, causing me to take another look to see what I had missed. And of course the same thing was true when the boys or girls from Art Cloth were attracted to someone from McAdenville or Lowell or Smyre. We were learning our first lessons in social intercourse, and by the end of the first semester we were all just classmates, without regard to where we lived.

I approached my first year of high school all full of pep and vinegar, determined to make straight "A"s and finish the four years at the top of the class. To graduate we were required to earn a certain number of credits, most of them on required subjects such as English, Math and Science, with the rest being electives. It averaged out to four required subjects and one elective per year. Since there were seven periods in the day, that left room for two study periods, or "Study Halls" as they were called, each day. I signed up for five required subjects and one elective my freshman year.

With only one Study Hall per day, I had to do quite a lot of studying at home, which didn't leave much time for extra-curricular activities. However, although my hormones were beginning to become quite active, I hadn't got really interested in any one girl yet, so I was able to keep up with my studies. But that would soon change.

Our high school only had two athletic teams, baseball and basketball. Being a small school in a low income community, we couldn't afford the uniforms and equipment to field a football team. I had played a lot of "pick-up" baseball when I was growing up, but I was never really very good at it. I guess I just wasn't very well coordinated, as the ball never quite seemed to meet the bat solidly when I swung, and somehow fly balls managed to elude my glove. So I went out for basketball.

I turned out to have a certain talent for it, although my lack of height handicapped me during my freshman year. We didn't have Junior Varsities in those days, so freshmen were eligible to play on the Varsity teams. But most of the players were sophomores, juniors or seniors, and had the advantage of having achieved much more of their growth. I didn't make the team that first year, although my friend Red Padgett did. But I was selected as Team Manager and got to travel with the team to all the games and sit on the bench with them.

Being Team Manager had another fringe benefit. We also had a Girls' Team, and both boys and girls played their games against the same schools on the same nights. For "away" games the teams were transported to the other town by parents who volunteered to drive them, and I usually managed to get myself in the back seat of a car next to one of the girls that I had a crush on at the moment. And after a particularly exciting game it was not unusual to get in a little surreptitious petting on the way home.

By about the middle of our Freshman year some of the members of our class had formed little groups of boys and girls who hung around together during recesses, study halls and after school. I found myself in one of them with another boy from Art Cloth named Jack Livingston, a boy from Lowell named Bobby Randall, Louise Wilson, Sue Ellen Snow , and Aleen Kendrick from Lowell. Outside of school, the principal meeting place for our Group was the First Methodist Church of Lowell. Aleen lived about half way between Lowell and Gastonia and went to high school in Gastonia, so she wasn't in our class. But she attended the Methodist Church in Lowell, so she became a member of our Group.

I had joined the Baptist Church in Art Cloth when I was twelve years old, having been caught up in the fervor generated one evening by a visiting Evangelist, and coming down front to be Saved. I was Baptized by immersion in the baptismal tank at the Lowell Baptist Church, since our Art Cloth Baptist Church cum schoolhouse didn't have one, and I attended Sunday School and Sunday evening Baptist Young Peoples' Union more or less regularly until I went to high school.

Since all the other kids in our "gang" went to the Lowell Methodist Church, I started going there, too. I even went so far as to go into Charlotte one Saturday and spend some of my savings on a new suit and a pair of Thom McAn shoes, so that I wouldn't feel out of place with the "rich" kids from Lowell. The Methodists had a young peoples organization similar to the Baptists' B.Y.P.U., and we used that as a meeting place on Sunday evenings. Afterwards we would either go to one of the Lowell kid's houses and play music and talk, or just walk around town if the weather was nice.

We had an even number of boys and girls in the Group, but nobody really "went" with anybody else, although Louise and Jack did have a bit of a thing going for a while. We just all pal-ed around together, and when we went to a dance or a sports event, any girl might be any one of the boys' "date". And even when we got older and some of us had a fling with someone outside our circle, the Group stayed together and didn't let it affect us.

By the end of that first high school year I had fallen in (and out of) love with a girl from Lowell who was not a member of the Group, gained almost two inches in height, and managed to pass all my subjects with at least a "B" average.

23

Running Away From Home Again

The summer of nineteen-thirty-eight didn't start off very well for me. I guess I was going through that period of adolescence often called "growing pains", when a boy's libido is exerting more and more control over his body. Whatever the reason, I seemed to be short tempered and irritable most of the time, and especially with my ten-year old brother, Wallace. Things came to a head one day in June when Mama gave me a whipping with her hickory switch for something that Wallace had done.   After brooding over life's unfairness for an hour or two, I decided to run away from home.

The only thing tying me down was the paper route, and Wallace could handle that. He knew all the customers from helping me out, and it would serve him right to have to do it all by himself. But the next question was, where would I go?   Then I thought of Daddy's sister, Aunt Perditta, and her husband, Uncle Mac Edwards, who lived up in the mountains near Highlands, North Carolina. That would be a great place to spend the summer, and Mama wouldn't think of looking for me there! I had only been to Aunt Perditta's once before, and that was when I was about five years old and living on the farm at Fountain Inn, South Carolina, and Daddy had the Model "T" Ford. But I had been to the Boy Scout Camp at Tryon, which wasn't too far from Highlands, and I had a map of North Carolina in my Boy Scout knapsack, so I was sure I could find it.

After giving it some thought I decided to leave after supper and hitchhike to Shelby and spend that first night at Ella Mae's house. As near as I could figure it was about a hundred miles from Shelby to Highlands and I should be able to make that in one day. There weren't many cars on the road in those days, but people were more inclined to pick up hitchhikers than they are today. It all sounded much easier than it actually turned out to be.

After supper I went to the room that I shared with Wallace and one of the boarders and packed my Boy Scout knapsack with extra socks, underwear, and my Boy Scout cap, figuring that it would be easier to catch a ride if I had it on. Mama was in the kitchen cleaning up the supper dishes, and when she asked where I was going I told her I was going down toward the river at Penhook to work on a Boy Scout Merit Badge. I did start out in that direction, but as soon as I was out of sight of the house I cut across behind the mill, crossed the P&N tracks and came out on the road to Lowell. I walked through Lowell, detouring around the middle of the town, and on out about a mile to the highway that ran from Charlotte to Gastonia, Kings Mountain and Shelby.

I got a ride to Gastonia right away and about an hour later, just as it was getting dark, an elderly couple in an "A" Model Ford picked me up and gave me a ride all the way to Shelby. I told them I was going to visit my sister, which was true, as far as it went, and they dropped me off just a few blocks from Ella Mae's house.

If my big sister was surprised to see me, she didn't show it. With five brothers, and three boys of her own at that time, she knew just about all there was to know about boys. And I'm sure she quickly figured out that I was running away from home. But she didn't come right out and ask me if I was, just asked me if I had come to stay with her and Woody and the boys for a while. I told her no, that I was on my way to Highlands to spend the summer with Uncle Mac and Aunt Perditta. She said that would be nice, but I had better stay there with her that night and get a good rest for my trip. Of course I agreed, and after eating some more supper at her insistence, I climbed in bed with Bob and went to sleep.

I didn't know it at the time, but as soon as I went to bed Woody went out to a nearby store and called Lowell to let my Mama know where I was. We didn't have a telephone in those days. In fact, outside of the grocery store and drug store, there was only one telephone in the village of Art Cloth. That one was in the home of Mr. Brownley, the Superintendent of the mill. But he and his wife were very good about taking and delivering important messages for the people of the village, so Mama didn't lose any sleep over me that night.

I was up bright and early the next morning, and after a good breakfast I was out on the highway with my Scout cap on and my thumb extended in the classic hitchhiker's position. I had pretty good luck at first, and by noon I was all the way to Chimney Rock, where the road forked and one branch headed west toward Hendersonville, Brevard and Highlands. Ella Mae had fixed me a sandwich, so I sat down beside the road and ate my lunch. Then I walked for a while to stretch my legs before hitchhiking again. There weren't as many cars on this road and it was quite a while before I got a ride, and that was only for a few miles. It was a hot day, and by mid-afternoon I was tired and sweaty, and beginning to have some second thoughts about running away from home.

But this wasn't like running away to Dallas, and I couldn't just turn around and be back home in an hour. So I kept going and pretty soon I got a nice long ride with two college students who were going to summer school, and they took me all the way to the college town of Brevard. From there I managed to get a ride with a farmer in a "T" Model truck, and he took me about halfway to Highlands before he turned off.

It gets dark early in the mountains, as the sun goes down behind the peaks, and although I didn't have a watch I figured it was about six o'clock as I walked along the road. I hadn't seen a car for almost an hour, and as the shadows deepened into dusk I began to get scared. My Mama and Daddy had been born and raised in these mountains, and I remember them telling stories of wildcats, "painters" as they called them, attacking people and carrying off small animals and even babies. I had my Boy Scout knife in my knapsack, and I got it out and cut myself a strong stick off of a limb of a dogwood tree alongside the road. I didn't know how much protection it would be against painters, but it felt reassuring in my hand.

By now it was almost dark, and there wasn't a light to be seen anywhere. I mentally kicked myself for running off in such a hurry and not planning a little better. At least I should have brought a flashlight and a warm jacket. When the sun set the temperature had dropped rapidly, and I was shivering in my thin shirt. If I had seen a house or a cabin, or any sign of human habitation, I would have gone to it and asked for shelter for the night. But there was nothing, just me and the mountains and the lonely road.

The pine trees were thick along both sides of the road, with a solid blanket of needles beneath them. I remembered from my Boy Scout training that pine needles made good insulation, and was giving some thought to lying down under the trees and covering myself with needles to try to keep warm, when I saw a glimmer of light back down the road in the direction from which I had come. Within seconds I could see that it was the headlights of a car. Not wanting to take a chance that it might pass me by without stopping, I stepped into the road and started waving my arms frantically. As it got closer I could see that it was a truck of some sort, and as the driver squealed his brakes I jumped out of the way to keep from getting hit.

The driver let out a few choice words and asked me what the blankety-blank I thought I was doing. Did I want to get myself killed? Then I guess he got a good look at me and saw that I was just a boy, for he calmed down and asked me what I was doing out here alone at night, and where I was going. When I said I was going to my uncle's at Highlands he told me to get in. He wasn't going all the way to Highlands, but the could take me to a truckers rest stop about ten miles from there. I could spend the night there and try to get a lift to my Uncle Mac's the next morning.

Compared to the outside air, the cab of the truck was nice and warm, and I soon fell asleep and didn't wake up until we turned in to the truck stop. The driver, whose name was Bill, parked the truck and told me to come on with him and get some supper in the truck stop cafe. I told him I didn't have any money, but he said he would treat me. When we got inside Bill told the owner behind the counter where I was going. The owner knew my Uncle Mac, and said I could sleep in the truckers' bunkhouse that night, and get a ride with the Mailman the next morning. He would be going right by Uncle Mac's house.

I was almost starved, but I didn't want to overdo a good thing, so I just had a hamburger and a glass of milk. It was about the best hamburger I ever had. Bill had a full meal, the Blue Plate Special, and when he finished he took me out to the bunkhouse. It wasn't really a bunkhouse, as it didn't have any bunks. It was a rectangular shaped wooden building, about 20' by 30', and had one big room with twelve single cots lined up in three rows of four, and a bathroom with toilets, wash basins and showers across one end. I picked out an empty bunk and put my knapsack on it. Bill said he lived just a mile or so down the road so he was going on home. I thanked him very much and told him so-long.

My spirits, which had been at a low ebb only an hour or so ago, were now rising and this whole episode was beginning to seem like an adventure again. Back in the bunkhouse I took a long hot shower, enjoying the unaccustomed luxury of all the hot water I wanted, then fell into bed and went right to sleep.

I was awakened the next morning by the sound of truck engines revving up, as the truckers pulled out of the parking area and hit the road. After washing up and getting dressed I went over to the cafe and told Mr. McCabe that I would be glad to work for some breakfast, washing dishes or cleaning the bunkhouse or anything else that he needed done. He said that he had regular help who did those things, but he'd fix me some breakfast anyway, and by the time I finished the mailman would probably be coming by.

He hit it right on the head. Just as I was sopping up the last bit of egg on my plate with the last piece of biscuit, a car with the words, "U. S. Mail" lettered on its sides pulled up in front of the cafe. A big man in gray pants and shirt, with the same lettering on the shirt pocket, got out and came in. Mr. McCabe introduced him to me as Mr. Jed Garrett. I asked him if he could give me a ride to Mr. Mac Edwards place and he said sure, just as soon as he had a cup of coffee and a piece of Mrs. McCabe's famous apple pie.

It took almost two hours to cover the ten miles from the truckstop to Uncle Mac's, with the mailman having to turn off the main road every few minutes to deliver mail to a house or cabin around a mountainside or down a holler. Although I was anxious to get there, I didn't mind the detours.   The scenery was beautiful and some of the mountain cabins looked like the ones I imagined Mama and Daddy living in when they were little. It was almost like being transported back about fifty years in time.

When we were a couple miles from Highlands Mr. Garrett turned off onto a dirt road that wound around for a half mile or so before heading down into the valley where Uncle Mac had his farm on two hundred acres of land that was completely surrounded by a National Forest.   As we rounded a bend in the road the house and outbuildings came into view.

The house was big for a mountain dwelling. It had two stories, with the first story constructed of stone and the second from rough hewn heavy timbers and logs. I learned that it was more than a hundred years old, having been built by Uncle Mac's grandfather, who was one of the first white settlers in the area. The stone in the first story was field stone collected when the fields were cleared for planting, and used to fortify he house against attacks by hostile Indians.

Some distance from the house there was a barn and another smaller building with a big wheel taller than the building next to it. I could see that the wheel was turning slowly and that water was pouring out of troughs in it as it reached the bottom of its turn.   Although I had never actually seen one, I had seen pictures of them and realized that it was a waterwheel. As we came closer I could see a small lake or pond on the other side of the house.

Mr. Garrett stopped in front of the house and blew his horn. A short, stout woman who looked to be about fifty years old came out on the front porch and down the steps. She had gray hair that was combed back smooth over her head and fastened in a bun at the back, and a smooth round face that seemed to smile all over. Her one piece print dress that buttoned down the front was protected by a big flowered apron tied at her ample waist, giving her the appearance of a Norman Rockwell painting of somebody's grandmother in the "Saturday Evening Post." Even though it had been almost ten years since I had seen her, I knew it had to be Aunt Perditta.

I got out of the car and started to tell her who I was, but before I could say a word she wrapped her arms around me and gave ma a big hug and said, "Why, you must be one of Sidney's boys. Which one are you?" I told her I was Sidney, Jr., and she said, "I should have known it, I declare, you look just like him. Why you must be hungry after that long trip. Come on inside and let me get you something to eat. Your Uncle Mac and Cousin Virginia have gone into Highlands to pick up some things, and Bruce and Eric are working at their sawmill. They'll be home for their dinner directly."

I thanked Mr. Garrett for the ride, then got my knapsack and followed Aunt Perditta into the house. It didn't dawn on me to wonder why she wasn't surprised to see me, or how she guessed that I was one of Daddy's sons, since she had quite a few nephews. It wasn't until I found out that they had a telephone that I began to put two and two together.

In spite of the fact that it was beginning to get hot outside, the inside of the stone house was pleasantly cool. The first floor had a living room with a big fireplace, a dining room with a table that would seat at least eight people, a big kitchen with a wood burning cook stove that looked just like Mama's, and two bedrooms and a bathroom. The second floor, when Aunt Perditta took me to show me where I would be sleeping, had four more bedrooms and a bathroom. Opening the door to one of the bedrooms that had two single beds, she said that this was her youngest boy John's room, but he was away for the summer, working as a counselor at a Boy's Camp over near Franklin. He was seventeen years old and would be going off to college at Cullowhee in the fall. She showed me which bed to take and where to put the few things I had in my knapsack.

We got back downstairs just as Uncle Mac and Virginia were pulling in from Highlands. Right behind them Bruce and Eric drove up in their truck from the sawmill. I was introduced to all of them, and when everybody had washed up we sat down to dinner.

Aunt Perditta sure set a good table. There were fried pork chops, ham, boiled potatoes, turnip greens, corn, biscuits and gravy, iced tea, and cold milk right from the spring house. And for dessert there were two kinds of pie. At first I thought maybe this was a "welcoming" dinner for me, but I soon learned that this was everyday fare at the Edwards' table. Of course, they ate their big meal at noontime, since the men had been hard at work since sunrise.

During dinner I learned more about their family. Aunt Perditta and Uncle Mac had eleven children, eight boys and three girls. All of them were grown, with families of their own, except the four still at home; Virginia, Eric, Bruce and John. Virginia was the oldest, probably about thirty-five. She was a graduate of the State Teacher's College at Cullowhee, and taught school in Highlands. She had never married. Eric was twenty and would be a senior that fall at North Carolina State University at Raleigh. Bruce was eighteen, and didn't plan to go to college. Since graduating from high school he had helped his Daddy on the farm until he started the sawmill.

Uncle Mac didn't really farm much now. He had two cows for milk and butter, raised some hogs and beef cattle for meat for the table, and had laying hens for eggs and

Aunt Perditta

fryers for eating. He also had two mules which he used for planting a few acres of corn and hay to feed the stock. The thing he enjoyed most now was his vegetable garden. He always planted about an acre of rich land near the house in sweet corn, beans, tomatoes, potatoes, turnips, and just about every other vegetable that you could imagine. What the family didn't eat right away, Aunt Perditta put up in half gallon fruit jars for later consumption.

Their farm sat right in the middle of several thousand acres of National Forest. In addition to the usual pine and fir trees, the forest contained a lot of hardwoods, including chestnut trees. The area around Highlands was one of the favorite places for wealthy Northerners to build summer homes, and chestnut lumber was very much in demand for interior paneling. In the early nineteen thirties some sort of blight struck the chestnut trees and hundreds of them died. Bruce got the idea of harvesting these dead trees and applied to the U. S. Forestry Service for permission to cut them.

When they gave him permission he borrowed money from his Daddy to buy a saw, carriage and a Dodge automobile engine, and set up his sawmill on Uncle Mac's land, as close as he could get to the dead chestnuts. He hired a local black man to help him, and with Eric's help in the summer and John working with him after school, he cut down the trees, hauled the logs to his mill, and sawed them into boards which he sold to the local lumber yard. His business grew rapidly and soon he was hard put to keep up with the demand for his chestnut lumber.

After we finished dinner Bruce asked me if I would like to see his sawmill. When I said I would, Virginia offered to drive me there and bring me back.

I don't know what I was expecting, but at first sight the sawmill wasn't very impressive. It was just a long open shed with a tin roof. Under the roof was the Dodge engine, with one drive belt running from the crankshaft to the big circular saw, and another system of gears that moved the carriage back and forth so that the log on it was sliced cleanly into boards by the spinning teeth of the saw blade.

Directly underneath the blade of the saw was a sort of pit with a ramp made of boards leading up out of it, and in the pit was the biggest wheelbarrow I had ever seen. It had a wheel at least four feet in diameter, and sideboards that gave it a capacity of at least a cubic yard. As I watched I could see that it was rapidly filling up with sawdust, and another almost identical wheelbarrow was sitting at the ready at the top of the pit. I didn't know it at the time, but I would get to know these 'barrows' intimately before the summer was over.

Bruce proudly explained the workings of his mill, and then asked me if I would like to earn some money by working there that summer. When I asked what my job would be, he told me that I would be the "wheelbarrow man". All I would have to do was wait for a wheelbarrow to fill with sawdust, pull it out from under the saw, put the empty one in its place, then run the full one up the wooden ramp and dump it at the top of the sawdust pile. Then keep repeating the procedure. For that, he said, he would pay me a dollar a day. That sounded like pretty easy money to me, so I said I would do it. He told me I could start the next morning.

I was very curious about the waterwheel, and as Virginia drove me back to the house I asked her how it worked. When we got back she took me out and explained it to me. As a work of engineering it was really very simple.

The waterwheel itself was about twelve feet in diameter and three or four feet wide. Two sets of wooden spokes as big around as a man's arm, one set on each side, supported curved wooden rims and a series of "V" shaped wooden troughs. A small clear cold stream flowed down the hillside from the nearby mountains, and when you wanted the wheel to turn you diverted the water from the stream into the top trough by moving a wooden sluice. When the top trough filled, its weight caused the wheel to turn so that the water ran into the next trough and so on. As the filled troughs reached the bottom of the wheel they emptied back into the stream, which then ran under the wall of the springhouse before flowing out the other side and on down the hill to the pond that I had seen at the other side of the farmhouse. In the process, the cold water chilled the milk and apple cider, and anything else that was in the wooden sided springhouse box.

The wheel revolved on a well greased axle. An extension at one end of the axle penetrated the side of the springhouse and connected to a series of gears inside.

These gears worked much like the gears on a bicycle, so that when the last one engaged the spindle of a generator it caused the spindle to turn at hundreds of revolutions per minute and generate electrical current. This current was fed into big storage batteries which in turn powered the electric lights, water pumps, and anything else electrical around the house. I imagine it was a little more complicated than that, but that's the way Virginia explained it to me so that I could understand it.

The pond on the other side of the house served as a catch basin for the water from the springhouse. When the water reached a certain level it spilled over into a stream that ran on down the valley to a larger stream below. The water in the pond was too cold for swimming, even during the heat of the summer. But there were fish in it, and a lot of bullfrogs. The banks of the pond were covered with a brushy growth and the big leaves of water lilies floated on its surface. At night the bullfrogs made an infernal racket, but when Aunt Perditta wanted froglegs for dinner it was easy to get a good mess of them by going along the bank after dark, shining a flashlight in the frogs' eyes and sticking them with a frog gig.

I slept like a log that night in a feather bed with the cold mountain air coming in through an open window, and the next morning I was up at daylight, ready for my first day at the sawmill. I hadn't brought any work clothes with me, so Aunt Perditta gave me a pair of John's bib overalls and a work shirt. The overalls were a couple sizes too big for me and I had to tighten the shoulder straps as far as they would go and turn up the bottoms of the legs two or three inches. I couldn't wear any of John's shoes, so I had to make do with the tennis shoes I had worn when I left home.

After a real lumberjack's breakfast, we set out for the sawmill in Bruce's truck. When we got there Bruce started the Dodge engine, and while Eric and the Colored man, Efrem, wrestled the first log of the day onto the carriage, Bruce showed me how to handle the wheelbarrows. The last one from the day before was still in the pit and was about half full of sawdust. To begin to break me in easily, Bruce told me to pick up the handles and run it up to the top of the sawdust pile and dump it. As soon as I was clear of the pit he put the second wheelbarrow in it. With the 'barrow being only half full, and the sawdust having lost some of its moisture overnight, this first trip up the hill wasn't too bad, although it was harder than I had thought it would be.

Bruce stayed with me for an hour or so, and after each trip he let the wheelbarrow in the pit fill up a little more before I took it. At the same time he showed me how to replace the full one with the empty one without losing too much of the sawdust into the pit. By the time he left me alone with it, I could handle a wheelbarrow three quarters full and make the switch to the empty one with a minimum of wasted motion. But it wasn't long before my back and arms were aching, and I was sure I was getting blisters on my hands, in spite of the big leather gloves Bruce had loaned me.

Luckily for me it was Saturday, and they only worked the sawmill five and a half days a week. Saturday afternoon was for doing odd jobs around the farm and going into Highlands to shop or just loaf around. Sunday was a day of rest and going to Church, if you wanted to.

The Edwards family were not very strict churchgoers. Virginia and Aunt Perditta went most of the time, and Uncle Mac and the boys went now and then. Mostly the boys just took it easy, resting up from a hard week's work and getting ready for the next one. I found it easy to go along with that routine. And if I got a little bored there were always blue gill and bass to fish for in the pond.

I liked both of the Edwards boys that I had met, but Bruce was my favorite. Eric took after his Daddy, tall and thin and rather quiet. Bruce, on the other hand, looked more like Aunt Perditta. He was about five feet ten inches tall, and while there didn't seem to be an ounce of fat on him, he was stockily built, with square shoulders and big muscular arms and legs. He had an outgoing personality and I found it very easy to talk to him. He didn't talk down to me as if I were a child, but treated me like an equal.

That first Saturday afternoon Bruce took me into Highlands and bought me a pair of overalls that fit, a couple work shirts, a pair of work shoes and a farmers straw hat to keep the hot sun off my head in the sawdust pit. He also bought me a pair of soft leather work gloves. When I had taken off my gloves after that first morning's work, I had two blisters on my hands, and some other places that were ready to blister. Aunt Perditta put some cream on them that soothed them. She said it would also help dry up the blisters and I should be all right by the time we went back to work on Monday.

143

I was real pleased with the clothes and told Bruce to take the cost of them out of my wages, but he said it was part of his cost of operating his business, and that I could do more work if I was dressed right for it. That night Aunt Perditta also rubbed my back and shoulders with some of her homemade lineament. It smelled pretty bad, but it did help and I felt much better the next day.

I asked Aunt Perditta if it would be all right if I stayed with them for the rest of the summer. She said it would be, on one condition – I had to write Mama and tell her where I was. I was pretty sure she already knew, but I said I would. And since there was no use putting it off, I sat down and did it. I was still kinda mad over the whipping, so I didn't say much, just told her where I was and that I was okay and would be staying until school started. Aunt Perditta took the letter and said she would give it to the mailman on Monday.

Virginia and Aunt Perditta went to Church Sunday morning, and while Bruce and Eric got a couple extra hours of well deserved sleep I helped Uncle Mac with the chores. We milked the cows (he was surprised that I knew how to milk), fed the mules and chickens and slopped the hogs. He let me move the sluice and start the waterwheel turning to add a little more charge to the storage batteries, then we went inside the springhouse and I got a drink of some ice cold sweet apple cider right out of the springhouse box. It was delicious! Uncle Mac was a quiet man, something like my Daddy, but as we did the chores together he opened up quite a bit and told me more about his family and how they came to settle in this mountain valley.

After the womenfolk got home from Church they fixed a big Sunday dinner and I ate so much I almost popped. After dinner I had a chance to talk some more to Virginia. She taught English and English Literature at Highlands High School. As might be expected, she was an avid reader and had quite a library of books at home. She seemed very pleased to find that I liked to read, and asked me all about the kind of books I liked. We had some very interesting talks during the rest of the summer. Among other things, she introduced me to Shakespeare's works, which we hadn't studied yet in my class at Lowell High. The way she explained them, I found them fascinating, especially "Julius Caesar" and "MacBeth". Looking back now, I see that I went to Summer School that summer, without even realizing it.

Monday morning found me back in the sawdust pit at the sawmill. Aunt Perditta's lineament had helped my aching muscles, and my hands felt much better inside the new softer gloves. I settled into a sort of rhythm of pulling out the full wheelbarrow, replacing it with the empty one, then running it up the sawdust pile and emptying it and getting back before the next one was full. After a while I reached a pace where I could even get a couple minutes rest between trips. It took a few days to toughen my muscles and build calluses instead of blisters on my hands, but by the end of the week I was a seasoned "sawmill hand".

The next Saturday night Bruce and I went to a Barn Dance in Highlands.

To cater to the rich northerners who came there just for the summer, the City of Highlands had built a barn-like structure just off the main square of the town, and dances were held there every Saturday night during the summer season. I didn't know the first thing about barn dancing, but Bruce said there was nothing to it and I would catch on to it in no time. And besides, there were sure to be some pretty little teenage northern girls there for me to dance with. I suspected that Bruce was more interested in the pretty eighteen or nineteen year olds that would be there, but I agreed to go along.

After supper we spruced ourselves up and I put on my best clothes, and we set out for Highlands in Bruce's truck. Before we reached the main highway he said he had to make a stop on the way. Turning off onto a side road, he wound around the side of the mountain for what seemed like miles before pulling up in front of a rather rundown looking cabin.

We got out of the car and he knocked on the door. An old mountaineer in overalls and no shirt answered the door and shook hands with Bruce and we went inside. When Bruce gave him fifty cents he went over to one corner of the cabin's one room and lifted up a floor board. Reaching through a hole in the floor, he brought out a quart fruit jar filled with an almost colorless liquid, with just a faint tinge of yellow. Bruce took the jar and shook hands with the man again and we went out and got back in the truck.

When we were out of sight of the cabin Bruce pulled over and stopped the truck and opened the lid on the jar. Taking a good swig of the moonshine, he wiped his mouth with the back of his hand, then handed the jar to me, warning me that I couldn't drink the whiskey, he just wanted me to take a small sip to see what it was like. I did, taking a very small sip, just enough to wet my tongue.

And that was enough! When it hit the back of my throat it burned like fire and tasted like Aunt Perditta's lineament smelled. He didn't have to worry about me drinking that stuff! But then maybe that was his idea in giving me a little sip. He left the fruit jar in the truck when we got to the dance, as any kind of alcohol was strictly forbidden inside the barn. But a couple times during the evening I missed him for a few minutes and suspected that he was out in the truck having a drink, or smooching, or both.

The Barn Dance did turn out to be a lot of fun, and there were some girls there about my age. I was timid about dancing at first, but after a while I got into the spirit of things and began to "dosey doe" and "swing your partner" as if I knew what I was doing. Bruce had paid me my wages for the week and I was feeling rich, so I bought one of the girls a Coca Cola and we sat outside on a bench, talking and holding hands.

She was from up North and a year or two older than me, and would probably have let me do a little more than hold hands if I hadn't been so naive and inexperienced. Anyway, I had a good time and felt very grown-up, going to a dance with my eighteen year old cousin. I was a little bit worried that Bruce might drink too much and have trouble driving, but it didn't seem to bother him, and we got home after the dance with no problem.

The next few weeks were more or less like the first, although we didn't go to another barn dance. I settled into a routine and the days flew by, and before I knew it there were only a couple weeks left before school would be starting. One day Aunt Perditta got a letter from Mama, saying that Daddy and my sister, Dot, would be up to get me and bring me home the next weekend. I had mixed feelings. I had really enjoyed the summer and hated to leave, but I was getting anxious to see my family and friends at home.

Daddy and Dot arrived Saturday afternoon. They would spend the night and we would leave for home Sunday morning. I didn't work at the sawmill Saturday morning, so Bruce paid me off Friday night. Except for a dollar or two in spending money, I had asked him to hold the rest of my pay and give it to me when I was ready to leave. When he counted it out that night I had thirty-five dollars to add to my college fund.

The ride home in Daddy's old Buick was faster and a lot easier than hitchhiking. As I relaxed and enjoyed the scenery, I couldn't help thinking that what had started out as a fit of pique on my part had turned into a pretty good summer.

24

My Sophomore Year

It was good to get back in school again and see the friends that I had missed by being away most of the summer. All of the members of our little Group were back, and we took up where we left off. Once again I signed up for an extra credit course, and as things turned out it was a good thing I did. I also went out for the basketball team again, and once again I failed to make it and ended up as Team Manager. But I did show progress. This time I was the last player cut from the ten man squad. Although I had grown about two inches in the last year, and was now five-feet-ten, so had a lot of other boys, and some of them were just a little bit better players that I was.

I won the consolation prize again and got to ride to the games with the members of the girls' team. Before a month had passed I had fallen in love with the big center of the team and managed to sit next to her in the back seat of her father's car. The only problem was that her Daddy was very protective of her and kept his rearview mirror aimed right at us, so the best we could do was hold hands. And since he was a very big man, even that was risky.

Although I didn't realize it at the time, things were happening in the rest of the world that were going to have a profound effect on my life. Adolph Hitler had come into power in Germany and war clouds were gathering over

Europe. But very few people in America paid any attention to it, least of all high school students like us.

The mills were running full time again as the Depression ran its course, and the men and women of Lowell and the rest of the country were too busy enjoying the improvement in their economic condition to worry about the prospect of a war in some far off part of the world. It did cross my mind that if the United States got into a war maybe I could get into the Army Air Corps without two years of college. But I was only fourteen years old, and if we got into a war it would probably be over before I was eighteen anyway.

Basketball season ended and with it my romance with the tall center on the girls' team. I was heartbroken for at least a week, but then I started looking around at the other girls in school and decided that she wasn't all that great looking anyway. And besides, there were other things besides girls. Like flying, for instance.

I still remembered every moment of that ride in the airplane with Tex Barnes. Although I was never lucky enough to get another free ride, I spent as much time as I could around the Charlotte airfield, just watching the planes take off and land. Once I even saw a big Ford Tri-Motor plane land at the airfield. I was dying to see the inside of it, but they put a guard on it and wouldn't let anyone go near it.

I devoured anything about flying that I could find to read, and started building model airplanes again. Mama had a full house of boarders so there wasn't much room anyplace for me to work. The models were made out of strips of balsa wood that were pinned down on a flat surface and glued together with model cement. So I used a heavy piece of cardboard and worked on the kitchen table in the evenings after Mama had cleared everything away from the evening meal, storing the unfinished model under my bed when I wasn't working on it.

My friend Red Padgett was also building model planes and we tried to outdo each other to see who could build the best ones. Sometimes we built "flying" models which were powered with a rubber band that you wound up by turning the propeller counter clockwise until the band had two or three rows of knots, one on top of the other. We would fly them off the top of the hill behind our house, and they usually ended up in a broken heap at the bottom. I can't say that we learned a lot about aerodynamics from these attempts at model flight, but we certainly learned perseverance.

I didn't do quite as well with my grades in my Sophomore year. After the excitement that came with just getting into high school, the second year was sort of a letdown. Then, too, I got interested in other things, like girls and flying. And shooting pool.

The little shopping center at Art Cloth was right on my way to school, and there was a pool table in the back room of the drug store. Somehow I got into the habit of stopping off on the way to school in the morning and shooting a game of pool with one or two of the men who hung around there. I got pretty good at it, and began to feel quite grown-up. Sometimes I would forget about the time and be late for school. This went on for quite some time, and when the men I was shooting with asked me if I didn't have to get to school by a certain time, I shrugged my shoulders and said I could get there when I wanted to.

Then one morning, just as I was bending over the pool table to make a tricky shot, I felt a hand on my head and fingers pinching my ear. "Put down that pool stick, young man, and get to school," Mama's voice announced for everyone in the pool room to hear. I was mortified at my Mama coming into the pool room to get me, and to add to my shame, she held onto my ear and marched me out the front door of the drug store.

Either someone had snitched on me, or my teacher had sent Mama a note about my tardiness. I was so embarrassed that I didn't go near the pool room for a long time, and I never stopped off there again on the way to school.

In spite of these distractions, I did enough work to pass all my subjects, with only one "C", and at the end of the year I was still two credits ahead of schedule on what was required for graduation.

That summer I did a lot of reading and spent quite a lot of time swimming in the pond behind Aleen's house. Her Daddy was an Engineer for the Gaston County Highway Department and they lived out in the country on New Hope Road, about halfway between Lowell and Gastonia.

Although Aleen went to Lowell Methodist Church, and was a member of our "Group", she had gone to high school in Gastonia for her first two years, but was planning to transfer to Lowell High for her Junior and Senior years. She had two sisters, one older and one younger, and their father had had the pond dug so that they would have a place to swim and entertain their friends. It was a popular place in the summertime, with a gang of kids always around, and was close enough to Art Cloth for me to ride my bike there and back.

Aleen and I had a little harmless flirtation going for a while that summer. We would horse around in the pond and do a little hugging in the water, then sit on her back porch and hold hands. But there was never anything really sexual about it. She seemed more like a sister to me, and was too nice a girl for me to think of her that way. It was all over by the time school started.

Daddy had planted a big garden that year and I helped him with it, putting into practice what I had learned on

Grandpa Ash's farm when I was eleven. I turned fifteen in June and had grown another inch in height, so I was sure I would make the basketball team that fall. After the hard work in Bruce's sawmill the summer before, I was pretty content to hang around home and take it easy.

I had patched things up with Mama by being especially helpful around the house, feeding her chickens and collecting the eggs, making sure she had a good supply of wood for her cookstove, and doing anything else I could to make things a little easier for her. She had Mrs. Williams to do the housecleaning and laundry, but insisted on doing all the cooking herself, and there were times when she looked very tired. We had never been a very demonstrative family, but sometimes I just felt like putting my arms around her and hugging her. Maybe I was having a premonition that there wouldn't be many more summers like this.

On September 1, 1939, just a week before I entered the tenth grade at Lowell High School, Hitler's armies invaded Poland. Three days later Britain and France declared war on Germany and World War II had begun.

25

Tenth Grade – An Apple For The Teacher, A Tackle For The Coach

I got a crush on our new Home Economics teacher, Miss Dorothy Turner, in the tenth grade. She and our new Biology teacher, Miss Ruth King, were fresh out of college and on their first teaching jobs. Miss Turner was pleasingly plump and pretty, with shoulder length black hair and sparkling brown eyes. But Miss King was beautiful. A tall statuesque blond, she had classic features, peaches and cream complexion, and a figure like a Greek goddess. Half the boys in the high school, and both the unmarried male teachers, fell instantly in love with her.

But not me. I found Miss King aloof and somewhat cold natured, while Miss Turner had a sparkling personality and a ready smile for everyone. Of course, I had Miss King for my teacher in Biology, and didn't take Home Ec from Miss Turner, which may have had some bearing on my feelings toward them.

Every afternoon after school and before basketball practice, I would find some excuse to stop by the Home Ec room and talk to Miss Turner. After I had done this a few times she started saving me cookies or whatever goodies her students had made that were fit to eat. Although I soon learned that she recognized my schoolboy-teacher crush for what it was, and was just trying to be kind to me, at the time I began to think that she had some romantic feelings for me. I found out differently about two months after school started.

Miss Turner's home was in Forest City, about fifty miles west of Lowell. She and Miss King roomed together at the teacher's boarding house during the week, but she went home to her parents' in Forest City most weekends. One Sunday afternoon in November I decided to hitchhike to Forest City and see her. Feeling very grown-up, as if I were going on a date, I put on my best shirt and pants and set out. I didn't have much trouble getting rides and it only took me a couple hours to get to her hometown. Apparently her father was a prominent local business man, for the first person I asked told me how to get to their house.

It was a beautiful big white two-story house, and when I knocked on the door Miss Turner answered it herself. I could tell by the expression on her face that she was surprised to see me, but she smiled that warm smile and said, "Why Sidney Bolick, what are you doing here? And all dressed up, too. Did you come calling on me?" I was too tongue tied to answer, so she said, "Well come on in and have some lemonade. It's hot out there."

I stammered something about it "being such a nice day that I decided to get out on the road and before I knew it I was in Forest City and decided to stop by and see her." I think I must have been blushing, my face felt so hot. She took me into the living room and introduced me to her mother and father, who were reading and listening to music on the radio. Then we went out onto a screened-in back porch where a cool breeze was stirring, and she got us both a glass of cold lemonade.

I had a reputation among my friends and classmates of being quite a talker, but for once in my life I was at a loss for words. However, she soon put me at ease and we

155

talked about school and basketball, and she asked me about my family and what I wanted to do when I finished high school. When she asked that, the floodgates opened and I told all about my love of flying and how I wanted to go to college for two years so that I could become a Pilot in the Army Air Corps. She thought that was a wonderful ambition and was sure I would achieve it.

Before I knew it, it was late afternoon and I said I had better be going so I could get home before dark. She said she was driving back to Lowell and would be leaving in a few minutes. I could ride with her if I wanted to.

If I wanted to! At that moment I couldn't think of anything I would like better.

She told her parents goodbye and I said I was pleased to meet them, and we left in her car. She was a good driver and we made good time, but she didn't talk much on the way back to Lowell, as if she had something on her mind.

About a block from her boarding house she pulled the car over to the side of the road and stopped. She told me that she could tell that I liked her a lot, and while she was flattered and thought I was sweet, she was too old for me, besides being a teacher in my school. She hoped we could be friends, and that I would still stop by to see her in the Home Ec room, but that I should find a girlfriend closer to my own age. Then, just before I got out of the car to walk the rest of the way home, she leaned across the seat, put her hand on my shoulder, brushed my cheek with her lips and said maybe we shouldn't tell anyone else about my coming to see her today. That would be our secret.

The touch of her hand on my shoulder and the faint scent of her perfume when she kissed my cheek was so intoxicating that I quickly forgot my disappointment at what she had said, and I practically floated down the P&N tracks on my way home. I didn't go by to see her at school for a few days, but then I realized that she was right, and I

156

started stopping up for my cookies after school again. And we did remain friends until I graduated.

I finally made the basketball team! On my third try I survived the cut and got a uniform! So what if I was the tenth man on a ten man team, and had to sit on the very end of the bench next to Coach Clemmer and run errands for him. I was on the team. I practiced with them after school, traveled with them to the away games, huddled with them on the sidelines during time-outs and celebrated with them on those rare occasions when we won.

And sometimes when we were way ahead or hopelessly behind, which was more often the case, I even got to play a few minutes. But my big moment came toward the end of the season against our arch rival, Mount Holly High School.

They had a big team and were giving our smaller boys a physical beating. Their giant Center was especially rough. Every time he got the ball he swung his elbows viciously from side to side, sending our guys flying in all directions, but the hometown referee never called a foul on him. Coach Clemmer was livid and yelled at the official until his voice was hoarse. Sitting beside him on the bench, I yelled right along with him, and started muttering, "put me in Coach, I'll tackle him, put me in Coach, I'll tackle him." Finally in his frustration, and without realizing what he was saying, he said, "Okay, Bolick, go in and tackle him."

I reported to the scorer's table and at the next break in play I went running in and tapped Tom Knowles on the shoulder and told him I was replacing him. He looked at me like I was crazy, but went to the bench and sat down. Before Coach Clemmer realized what was happening, play started again and the big Mount Holly Center got the ball. Before he had taken two steps I charged across the floor at him and threw a flying block with my whole body, right across his knees. He went down in a heap and lay there clutching his right knee and moaning. At first I thought I had really hurt him bad, but then he got up and started for me and I took off around behind Coach Clemmer. There was pandemonium for a few seconds, with the referee frantically blowing his whistle and about six players holding back the guy that I had just tackled.

When order was finally restored, the referee stopped the game and awarded it to Mount Holly on a forfeit. Those of us on the Lowell team didn't stop to take our usual after-game shower, but grabbed our street clothes and hurried to our cars and got out of town. For a few days I was a hero to the student body of Lowell High School, and "Put me in Coach, I'll tackle him", became our team's rallying cry. Unfortunately, that was my last game. The season ended and I didn't play the next year because I was working after school. But I had had my one proud moment of never-to-be-forgotten glory.

What with basketball and other extra-curricular activities, my grades fell off again that year and I ended up with a high "C" average. But I passed all my subjects, and going into my Senior year I only had to have three more credits to graduate, which would allow me to adjust my schedule so that I could work in the mill after school.

In Europe, Germany had invaded and conquered Belgium, Luxembourg and the Netherlands, and the British Army had been forced to evacuate its troops through the Belgian port of Dunkirk. Hitler then turned all his might against France, and the French government surrendered on June 22, 1940.

I watched these developments in the war closely, but it seemed to me that most other Americans didn't really pay much attention to them.

26

Rites of Passage

June 18, 1940, was my sixteenth birthday. During the past year Daddy had taught me to drive in his old Buick, so the week of June 18th I got my driver's license, and went to work as a Cloth Boy in the mill at Art Cloth. I worked on the second shift, from 3 p.m. to 11 p.m., so that I could keep working after I went back to school in the fall for my Senior year.

My job as a Cloth Boy was to remove the rolls of cloth from the looms when they reached a certain size, put them on a four wheeled cart, reattach the end of the cloth to another roller, and take the rolls to the Grading Room. It wasn't a complicated job, but it was a tiring one. The rolls weighed about fifty pounds each, and after eight hours of lifting and loading and unloading them, you knew you had been working. But I was making thirteen dollars a week, which was almost as much as my Daddy made, and after giving Mama five dollars a week for board, and putting six dollars in my college savings account, I still had two dollars for spending money. Which was almost a fortune to a sixteen year old in those days.

Mama had taken over the family finances by that time, and about the time I got my driver's license she traded our old 1932 Buick for a good used 1938 Chevrolet, and learned to drive it. I was real pleased with her new car, as I would be driving it to school that fall so that I could get home in time to go to work.

In August of 1940, the Battle of Britain began, as Hitler tried to destroy the Royal Air Force in preparation for an invasion of England. But his plans were thwarted by a small group of Spitfire and Hurricane Pilots who defeated his Luftwaffe. I read everything I could find in the newspapers about this air war, and started a scrapbook of pictures and stories that I had cut out. I remember one picture in particular, of a Flight Lieutenant Eric Locke, who had just shot down his fifteenth German airplane, making him the first RAF Triple Ace. In my mind he came to symbolize the typical brave RAF pilot.

When school started in September, I arranged my schedule so that I had my three classes between ten a.m. and two p.m. That way I could sleep in a little later in the morning, after working until eleven the night before, and leave school in plenty of time to change clothes, eat, and be in the mill at three. I did my studying and homework in the Study Halls between classes. So that I wouldn't get too tired to work or study, Mama let me drive her car to school. In addition to being convenient, it was a lot of fun, and I felt like a big shot, taking a bunch of kids for a ride at lunch time, It was amazing how friendly some of the girls got, even some who had never given me a second look before.

I worked in the mill from September of nineteen-forty until February of nineteen-forty-one, when Mama made me quit. Although I was only taking three subjects in high school, working in the mill and going to school began to take its toll on me. My grades began to slip. I was behind in the reports on my Chemistry experiments, and I was becoming nervous and irritable. One night I came home from the mill and went to bed, but couldn't go to sleep. Then I started to cry for no apparent reason, and couldn't stop. Mama heard me and came into my room and asked me what was wrong. When I told her that I didn't know, that I just felt like crying, she said, "That's it young man, no more working in the mill for you until after school's out."

Although I hated to lose the thirteen dollars a week, I was actually relieved to quit working. Now, for what was left of my Senior year, I could enjoy going to high school. Mama still let me drive the car, and I always had things to do and kids to do them with.

The war between England and Germany was still going on, and the air war over Europe continued unabated. I still devoured any news that I could find about the RAF, and one day I saw something in the Charlotte paper that would have a profound effect on my life. The article was about the Eagle Squadron, a group of American flyers who had joined the RAF and were serving in a special Spitfire Fighter Squadron.

Of course, there was no way that I could qualify for the Eagle Squadron. Those pilots were men who had already been flyers before the war, and each of them had hundreds of hours of flying time. But at the very end of the article a short paragraph caught my eye. It said that more and more young American men, high school graduates and college students, were going to Canada and joining the Royal Canadian Air Force for Pilot training.

As I read this I got very excited. Maybe this was a way that I could learn to fly without getting two years of college first! There was no address to write to for information, but I figured that if I wrote to the RCAF in the Canadian capitol of Ottawa, they would get it. I was taking typing as an elective that semester, so the next day in class I wrote to the RCAF, telling them that I was considering coming to Canada to join up, and asking them to let me know the requirements for acceptance for pilot training.

161

I didn't tell anybody about writing the letter, not even my parents or my friend, Red Padgett, as I didn't want to be embarrassed or take a lot of kidding if nothing came of it. But it was all I could do to contain myself as I waited for an answer.

Two weeks went by without a reply, and I was beginning to get discouraged. But then I came home from school one day and Mama told me I had a letter from Canada. It looked very official, with the RCAF crest in the top left hand corner of the envelope, and I quickly ripped it open. It was from a Squadron Leader Cecil Smith, Recruiting Officer. He thanked me for my letter, and enclosed a mimeographed sheet with details of the requirements for acceptance for Pilot Training, closing with the hope that they would see me soon.

I read the requirements quickly, and they didn't seem too tough. Applicants had to be at least eighteen years old, high school graduate, in good physical condition, and able to pass an aptitude and intelligence test. Everything looked okay except the age. I wouldn't be eighteen until June of 1942, more than a year away. But I figured I could work that out somehow. Maybe Daddy would sign an affidavit saying I was a year older than I actually was. The first step was to make sure that I didn't have any unknown physical defects.

I told Mama what I was thinking of doing. She wasn't too happy about it, but didn't put her foot down and say no. I don't think she believed I would really go through with it, and she was quite sure that Daddy wouldn't lie for me about my age. I couldn't resist telling Red Padgett about it, so naturally it was soon all over the school. The reaction of my classmates and friends was mixed; some of them seemed impressed, and others kidded me about it. Some even appeared to be a little envious.

I went to our doctor, Doctor Groves, and told him what I was going to do and the kind of physical I wanted. He gave me a very thorough going over, with special emphasis on my vision, equilibrium, color perception, and anything else he thought might be on a flight physical. Although I was a pound or two underweight, I passed everything else with flying colors. I assured him that I would put on a few pounds before I left for Canada.

Daddy was another story. While he wouldn't stop me from going to Canada if I had my heart set on it, he refused to lie for me about my age. I didn't have a birth certificate, as all such records in Macon County, Georgia had been destroyed in 1930 when the old courthouse burned down. The only record of my birth was in the family Bible, and I couldn't change that. Then one of my classmates, a nerdy little guy named Nate Daniels, came to my rescue. His father was a Notary Public, and Nate said he would "borrow" his father's Notary seal and notarize an affidavit, if I would type it up.

And that's what we did. I went into the typing classroom after school, and in my best high school legalese I typed an affidavit certifying that I didn't have a birth certificate, but that I was born in Oglethorpe, Georgia on June 18, 1922. I put my age ahead two years instead of one, since I wouldn't be seventeen until June 18th, and I might possibly be in Canada to enlist before then. I typed my Daddy's name at the bottom and Nathan signed it. Then he notarized it with his father's seal and I signed his father's name. It was a pretty crude effort, but as things turned out, it worked.

I think Doctor Grove's nurse must have told someone about the physical I'd taken, for word got around the school that I was really going to Canada, and I became a bit of a celebrity, or at least a novelty, to my peers. It even got me a few dates with a girl I had had a crush on since the second grade.

Dorothy Nell Hughes was a pretty little girl, who looked a lot like Shirley Temple. Her mother had died when she was very young, and she and her father lived with her older married sister. She was very smart in school, always getting straight "A's", and I worshipped her with unrequited love all the way through Grade School. By the time we reached High School I had given up any hope of her ever paying any attention to me.

And she hadn't, until I decided to join the RCAF. Then she started smiling at me in class and stopping in the halls to talk to me between classes. I was still driving Mama's car to school, and she went for rides with me at lunch time.

I was never quite sure whether she had decided she really liked me after all those years, or whether she just liked the idea of dating a boy who was going away to war. Or maybe she was trying to make some other boyfriend jealous. I suspect it was the latter, since she married an older boy named Leonard about a year after I went away. In any event, we "went together" for the rest of the school year. We went to the Drive-in movie and to the Belmont Drive-in for lunch, and I took her to the Junior-Senior Banquet, which was our substitute for a prom. I was also busy getting ready for my departure for Canada, so the time passed quickly.

Every year the Lowell High School Senior Class took a graduation trip to Washington, D. C. on a chartered bus, and spent three days and nights touring the Capitol. I planned to ride as far as Washington with them, then take a Greyhound Bus from there to Ottawa. A week before school was out I went to the bank in Gastonia and took enough money out of my savings account to buy some new clothes and pay for my bus ticket to Canada, with a little extra for expenses. I transferred the balance of the account over to Mama, since I wouldn't be using it to go to college.

The Lowell High School Class of 1941, all twenty-one of us, graduated on June 6th. Dorothy Nell Hughes was the Valedictorian and Aleen Kendrick the Salutatorian. After the graduation ceremonies Louise Wilson had a lawn party for us at her house. The next morning we left for Washington.

I said goodbye to Mama and the rest of the family at home, and Daddy drove me to where the bus was waiting at the high school. He didn't say much on the way there, but before I got on the bus we shook hands and he put his arm around my shoulder and hugged me. It was the first time I could remember him hugging me since I was five or six years old. I looked down at my feet to hide the tears in my eyes as I joined my classmates.

The trip to Washington took about ten hours, with a stop somewhere in Virginia for lunch. There was a lot of laughing and joking and singing on the way, and I tried to join in. But my mind was on the rest of the trip and what was waiting for me at the end of it. When we arrived in the Capitol I asked the driver to let me off at the Greyhound Station. I would have liked to spend the night in Washington with my classmates, but I was anxious to get going, and I couldn't afford to spend any of my money on a night out with them.

I said goodbye to all of them, and kissed Dorothy Nell. She promised to write to me after I got into the RCAF, but she never did.

My route to Ottawa took me through New York City, with a change of busses there. The bus for New York was leaving almost immediately, so I gave my suitcase to the driver and got aboard. The bus wasn't crowded, and I had a double seat to myself. As we left the District of Columbia and went north through Maryland, I tried to watch the

165

scenery.

But my mind wasn't on it, and when it began to get dark I dozed off with my head against the back of the seat next to me. Several times during the trip I woke up and looked out the window but couldn't see anything except darkness outside so I went back to sleep. But as we crossed the New Jersey Meadowlands and approached the Lincoln Tunnel, I became wide awake. I had never been in a big tunnel before, and I found it both fascinating and frightening. I was glad when we emerged on the New York side and turned into the West Side Bus Terminal.

I had heard a lot of stories about New York City, but nothing I ever heard had prepared me for the way it actually was. Big buildings, taller than my eyes could see, were nestled side by side on both sides of every street, and even at midnight the city was lit up like a county fair, with people scurrying around like ants in an ant hill. I would have liked to see more of it, but I didn't dare leave the bus terminal for fear of getting lost and missing my bus to Ottawa.

The bus driver gave me my suitcase and told me that the bus for Ottawa would be leaving in just over an hour from Gate Six. This gave me time to get something to eat from one of the several snack bars in the terminal, and at twenty minutes before departure time I was the first in line at the gate for boarding. I didn't have a whole double seat to myself this time, but I did have a window seat. By this time I had been riding buses for more than fifteen hours, and I was getting tired. Shortly after the bus pulled out I leaned my head against the window and went to sleep.

I must have been more tired than I thought, for in spite of the uncomfortable position, I slept soundly. When I woke up it was daylight, and the bus driver was announcing our arrival at Ogdensburg, New York. As the bus topped a little rise, I looked out and saw the broad expanse of the St. Lawrence River spread out before me.

And there across the water, its shoreline shrouded by the river's morning mists, was Canada.

Epilogue

Mama's Boarding House burned to the ground in the summer of nineteen-forty-six. Everything was lost, including the family Bible and Daddy's prized Seth Thomas clock. Mama was no longer taking in boarders, so only she, Daddy, and my youngest sister Dot, were in the house at the time. Thankfully, no one was hurt.

I had returned from the War in November of nineteen-forty-four, after going through pilot training in Canada, and flying with the Royal Air Force and the U. S. Eighth Air Force in England. I brought my new Canadian wife with me, and we stopped off in Lowell for three days en route to the Redistribution Center at Miami, Florida. Mama was still running her Boarding House, but she had only three boarders - a middle aged couple and a World War I veteran named John Moore, who had been there when I left for Canada.

Mama didn't look good. She was in ill health, suffering from the stomach ulcers she had had since I was a boy, and that had been aggravated by worrying about her sons, all five of us being in the war and in combat. Luckily, we all survived with only minor injuries, but the prescription drugs she had taken to relieve her pain and anxiety had taken their toll on her health.

After going through the Redistribution Center in Miami I was posted to Tyndall Field at Panama City, Florida, then to Homestead, Florida. When the war ended in nineteen-forty-five I was stationed at Hamilton Field, California, flying four-engine transport planes on the Pacific Run.

I didn't get back to North Carolina the next year, and it was my brother George who called me and told me about the house burning down. He said that Mama and Daddy weren't going to rebuild the house. They sold the land that it was on, and Mama and Dot had gone to live with Belle.

George had gotten married and was working for the Ford Agency in Gastonia. He and his wife had bought a house there and Daddy was living with them.

Over the years Mama's health got worse, and it was finally necessary to put her in a nursing home. But in spite of her failing health, and a series of small strokes, she lived to be ninety-six. Although her body wasted away, she never lost the indomitable spirit that had enabled her to face and overcome all the hardships and challenges of her long life. Her mind remained sharp right to the end, and according to the nurse who looked after her, she died peacefully in her sleep.

Daddy died of a heart attack in July of nineteen-seventy, at the age of eighty-three. When I went home for his funeral, George and I drove over to Art Cloth and looked at the old homestead at the corner of Black and Linebarger Streets.

A modern brick house had been built on the site of our old house, and the owners had landscaped the yard, planting a new lawn and new shrubs and trees. But the big magnolia tree that had shaded the front porch was still there, and there was corn and tomatoes and other vegetables growing in Daddy's old garden plot. George and I agreed that the place looked nice, and that esthetically it was an improvement over the way we remembered it from our childhood. But somehow it looked cold, as if something important was missing.

As I stood there looking out across the old gully at the bottom of the hill where I had flown my model airplanes, I began to imagine that I heard voices from long ago; Mama and Daddy, and Jake and Wallace, and my little sister Dot; Johnny Matthews, and Eudora and Alexandria, and all the other boarders who had been a part of our family for so long. I could see Daddy in his rocking chair by the radio, and catch the tantalizing smell of fried ham and biscuits and fresh brewed coffee as Mama worked at her stove in the kitchen.

Then, as the sights and sounds and smells began to fade, my body seemed to be suffused with a warm glow, and I was possessed with a strange inner peace, as if the spirit of Mama's Boarding House was reaching out, like the Phoenix rising from its ashes, to welcome me home.

CPSIA information can be obtained
at www.ICGtesting.com
Printed in the USA
FFOW02n1334271217
44280754-43819FF

9 781552 125175